YORK NOTES

General Editors: Professor A.N. Jeffares (*University of Stirling*) & Professor Suheil Bushrui (*American University of Beirut*)

Percy Bysshe Shelley

SELECTED POEMS

Notes by Alasdair D.F. Macrae

MA (EDINBURGH)
Lecturer in English Studies, University of Stirling

LONGMAN
YORK PRESS

YORK PRESS
Immeuble Esseily, Place Riad Solh, Beirut.

LONGMAN GROUP UK LIMITED
Longman House, Burnt Mill, Harlow,
Essex CM20 2JE, England
Associated companies, branches and representatives
throughout the world

First published 1983
Fifth impression 1993

ISBN 0-582-02296-7

Produced by Longman Singapore Publishers Pte Ltd
Printed in Singapore

Contents

Part 1

Introduction

The life of Shelley

Percy Bysshe Shelley was born on 4 August 1792, the only son of an aristocratic family in Sussex in the south of England. His father was a Member of Parliament and his grandfather was a wealthy landowner. After attending school at Eton, Shelley entered University College, Oxford in 1810, the year in which he published his earliest poems and two Gothic novels. The following year, he was expelled from Oxford for distributing a pamphlet on *The Necessity of Atheism* and he further outraged his family by marrying a sixteen-year-old girl, Harriet Westbrook, against the wishes of both families. His revolutionary ideals led him to write pamphlets and participate in projects which brought him under suspicion from government spies; *Queen Mab*, a long poem propounding these ideals, was issued in 1813.

By 1814 Shelley's marriage had broken down and in July he eloped to the Continent with Mary Godwin, then only seventeen years old. She was the daughter of William Godwin (1756–1836), the political theorist and novelist much admired by Shelley, and Mary Wollstonecraft (1759–97), the author of *A Vindication of the Rights of Women*. Shelley's financial difficulties were acute until his grandfather died in 1815 and he inherited a considerable amount of money in annual payments. In 1816 his first mature poem, *Alastor*, was published and his friendship with Lord Byron (1788–1824) began. The death by suicide of his wife, Harriet, allowed him to marry Mary. Political issues occupied much of his thinking and his revolutionary ardour was expressed in a long narrative poem, *The Revolt of Islam*, published in 1818. Among Shelley's friends at this stage were Leigh Hunt (1784–1859), the poet and radical journalist who, with his brother, edited the critical magazine the *Examiner*, and Thomas Love Peacock (1785–1866), the comic and satirical novelist; Shelley knew and admired the young poet John Keats (1795–1821) but they never became close friends.

By the time Shelley left England in 1818 to live in Italy, he had lost custody of the two children by his first marriage and his first child by Mary died a fortnight after it was born. Two further children were to die shortly after their arrival in Italy. The Shelleys seemed unable to settle in any place for long and they never experienced any lasting contentment. In the area around Pisa in Northern Italy, however, they established a circle of friends and Shelley seems gradually to have accepted his self-imposed exile. Because of his style of life and his published ideas, he was commonly branded by British opinion as an immoralist, an atheist and a political subversive. His friendship with the more notorious Lord Byron did not help his reputation and he encountered considerable problems in having his work published. *The Mask of Anarchy* (see p. 18) was finished in 1819 but not published until ten years after his death; his most sustained and closely argued essay on politics, *A Philosophical View of Reform*, was not published until 1920, a century after its composition.

In the final four years of his life, Shelley wrote his most considerable poems. He finished *Prometheus Unbound* in 1819 and saw it as his major achievement. His poems were enormously varied and included dramas, satires, lyrics, odes, an elegy, verse letters, translations from several languages, allegories and narratives. In 1821 he wrote 'A Defence of Poetry' to justify the central significance of poetry in civilised life.

On 8 July 1822 Shelley was drowned in his sailing boat on his return from having welcomed Leigh Hunt to Italy. His body was burned on the beach because of strict quarantine laws then in force.

In his personality Shelley was charming, very passionate, of a quick intelligence, moving always towards speculation and seeking overall patterns which could make sense of the particulars around him, an idealist but bitterly sensitive to the imperfections in human behaviour, outraged by cruelty and intolerance.

Intellectual background

During the eighteenth century, the attention of European philosophers was concentrated on two main subjects: the nature and limits of man's faculty of reason; and the basis and sanction of authority in the state.

John Locke (1632–1704) argued that the mind of a man is originally blank but receptive, and through his senses the world around him impresses itself on the mind. Reason is involved in the process of knowledge because it helps to compare and relate the different impressions. This view of the relationship between mind and the world outside the mind was challenged by Bishop George Berkeley (1685–1753) who argued that the world is known by men as it is seen (and, therefore, shaped) by their minds; Berkeley was concerned to show that the human mind, that part of men which connects them to God, has power over the material world. Although the two philosophers disagreed on the order in which perception and thought take place, they both claimed that the existence of God could be proved rationally. In both philosophers, human reason was valued as what made men superior to the beasts and what provided men with cultivated tastes and standards. Such a reliance on reason was brilliantly undermined by the

Scottish philosopher David Hume (1711–76), who exposed rationally the faults in both Locke's and Berkeley's reasoning regarding perception, reality, morals and the existence of God. Shelley was a keen reader of philosophy and in his poetry and prose he explores the interaction of mind and the material world. The sceptical arguments of writers such as David Hume appealed to him and a deeply sceptical mentality is apparent in much of his poetry. A more positive metaphysical element in Shelley's work came from his interest in the ideas of the Greek philosopher, Plato (428–347BC). Plato had argued that the temporal world is a poor imitation of the real world of perfect, eternal forms. According to Plato, men can know something of this reality through contemplation and in this reality all human ignorance and striving are cleared away.

The other subject which occupied the thoughts of theorists in the period leading up to Shelley concerns the social nature of man. Thomas Hobbes (1588–1679) had put forward a view of men in society based, he claimed, not on his wishes or speculations but on actual observation. Men, according to Hobbes, are self-seeking and unscrupulous; only through the imposition of laws backed up with power can they be protected from each other. John Locke took a more optimistic view and felt that men were more capable of reasonable behaviour and more amenable to rational persuasion. It was, however, the French-Swiss thinker Jean-Jacques Rousseau (1712–78) who presented a theory which completely contradicted that of Hobbes. 'Man is born free, and everywhere he is in chains' states the first sentence of *The Social Contract* (1761). Rousseau's claim that man is, by nature, good but that he is corrupted by the artificialities and inhibitions of society called into question the standard view of civilised man. The world of nature, the untutored child, spontaneous feelings, the individual – these are the valuable things, according to Rousseau's theory. His elevation of feelings coincided with David Hume's attack on the rational basis of moral and social attitudes characteristic of Locke and with the savage indictment of hypocrisy, superstition and intolerance by the French satirist Voltaire (pseudonym of François Marie Arouet, 1694–1778).

Rousseau's social philosophy contributed strongly to the intellectual ferment which was manifested in the French Revolution of 1789. Already, in the successful revolt of the American colonists against British rule, Europeans had seen the intoxicating force of the ideas of freedom and equality. They were able to argue that the old order was not an inevitable and unchangeable fact but one system of power which could be replaced by a redistribution of wealth and rights among the people. Two British writers who contributed to, and developed, this radical political thinking were Thomas Paine (1737–1809) and William Godwin (1756–1836). Both attacked the idea that a particular class, a royal family or an aristocratic order, had the right to rule over other people; both attacked the abuses endemic in existing forms of government and Godwin went as far as to argue that man could become perfect in a new kind of society. Neither saw a belief in God as rational or beneficial and both were labelled as dangerous and subversive by the British Government. The French Revolution and the wars which followed it preoccupied European countries until after the final defeat of Napoleon at Waterloo in 1815; in Britain there was considerable fear in conservative circles that the revolutionary ideas could spread to Britain where social inequality, poverty, a savage penal code, laxity in religious life, and corruption in government and the law, offered fertile soil for political agitation.

From the second half of the eighteenth century onwards, changes in land use and the advance of the Industrial Revolution introduced fundamental alterations to British society. There was an increasing concentration of the land into the hands of a small number of owners and thousands of people whose forebears had worked the land found themselves dispossessed and forced to seek employment either in the towns or in the British Empire overseas. This movement from the countryside was accelerated by the development of new machines, animal breeding methods and farming techniques as well as by the rapid changes taking place in transport and in the industrialisation of the towns. New processes in mining, metal working, the manufacturing trades, were made possible by the successful development of the steam engine by James Watt (1736–1819) in the 1760s. A network of canals, roads and later railways was built to facilitate the easy flow of men and goods. With a vast empire from which to derive raw materials and which provided a hugh market for the finished products, with supplies of coal readily available, Britain was in a unique position to profit from industrialisation. The profit, however, was achieved at a massive human cost and was not divided fairly among those whose efforts created it. The owners of the new factories and canals showed, in the main, scant regard for the welfare of their workers; the towns and cities of the north (near the coalfields) grew into areas of squalor and misery while the landed aristocracy and the emerging class of factory owners and managers became proportionately wealthy and could afford to live well away from the sources of their wealth. As the Industrial Revolution progressed, the contrast between the towns and the country became more marked; the simple life of the countrymen came to be seen as honest and nature untouched by men came to be regarded as clean and good.

Literary background

Shelley is often described as a member of the Romantic Movement. The term 'Romantic Movement' is not very helpful; there was no grouping of writers of the kind suggested by the name and Shelley, therefore, could not be described as a member. The term was devised after Shelley and most of the other so-called Romantic poets were dead. It is, however, true that the period from about 1770 to 1830 was a time of great activity and innovation in literature, not only in Britain but throughout Europe and particularly in Germany. In the single figure of the German writer, Johann Wolfgang von Goethe (1749–1832), can be seen many of the new directions taken by literature; he experimented with new forms, new areas of subject and, in the interaction between his own life and his writing, he manifested one of the most striking characteristics of contemporary writing. It was widely felt by writers that the literary fashions and conventions adhered to through much of the eighteenth century had become too rigid and narrow and that a more individual, less conformist style of writing was now called for. The events of the period – the movements of large numbers of people, urbanisation and industrialisation, but, most of all, the French Revolution with its slogans, hopes and failures – these events caused writers to seek a manner of writing appropriate to them.

In the sixty years from 1770 to 1830 the population of England almost doubled, communications improved nationally, newspapers and journals appealed to larger readerships, and people became more mobile in search of work. One of the consequences of these changes was that the poet became less clear as to his audience than he would have been in the eighteenth century. The audience for a writer could now extend beyond his own national boundaries and writers such as Voltaire, Macpherson (see below), Sir Walter Scott (1771–1832), Goethe and Lord Byron were read immediately in every country of Europe. For the poet in particular, this enlarged audience offered new possibilities of influence but, conversely, the danger of irrelevance to any society. Poets began to try to justify their writing of poetry and to speak more directly to more people. However, from seeing themselves as spokesmen, representatives of their communities, many poets began to see themselves as figures in isolation from, even in opposition to, the traditional community. Although William Wordsworth (1770–1850) asserted in his Preface to the second edition of the *Lyrical Ballads* (1800) that the poet 'is a man speaking to men', the image of the poet which emerged in the public mind was closer to the bardic, prophetic figure presented by William Blake (1757–1827) in his Introduction to *Songs of Experience* (1794) and by Samuel Taylor Coleridge (1772–1834) at the end of his poem 'Kubla Khan' (written about 1798, published 1816).

The questions Plato had raised concerning the source of creativity and the relation of art to reality were re-examined by all the major poets of this period. Is poetry a reflection of the world around the poet, a deft expression of what everyone sees but lacks the talent to put into words? Or is the poem a manifestation of some inspiration peculiar to the individual poet, a revelation of a truth beyond the ordinary grasp of most people? Generally, the poets of Shelley's time chose the second approach and saw themselves as engaged on a quest of discovery, a pursuit of understanding the world and their place in it. Rousseau, particularly in his *Confessions* (written 1765-70), gives the self, his own development and feelings, a central place in his work; and the autobiographical element is prominent in the poetry of the subsequent period. Although not published until after his death in 1850, Wordsworth's *The Prelude* ('on the growth of an individual mind') was substantially written by 1805 and remains as the major poem of its age. In the emphasis he places on his childhood, on natural phenomena as clues to the configurations of the human psyche, on the mystery he apprehends at the edge of his rational mind, Wordsworth enunciates the subjects which have dominated poetry since his time.

Paradoxically, this new concern with the personal experience of the poet coincided with an enlargement of the horizons of poetry. The attempt was made by poets ranging from William Blake to Shelley himself to see man whole, not just in terms of a social fashion or in his obedience to a specific religious doctrine, but as a part of the whole scheme of creation. Missionaries, explorers, scholars and what would now be called anthropologists published accounts of cultures from outside Europe and its Classical past. In 1760 the Gaelic-speaking James Macpherson (1736-96) began to publish what he claimed were 'Fragments of Ancient Poetry Collected in the Highlands of Scotland, and Translated from the Gaelic or Erse Language'. These fragments, however unauthentic, attributed to the Irish bard Ossian of the third century, fed a European appetite for the exotic, the unsophisticated and the rhapsodic, and the following generation of British poets displayed a marked fascination with bizarre, sensational and forbidden happenings. Blake and Shelley found more to excite their sympathy in the figure of Satan than that of God in *Paradise Lost* by John Milton (1608-74); the solitary rebel defying orthodoxy appears in Blake's Orc, Goethe's Faust and Byron's Manfred, as well as in Shelley's Prometheus. The poet saw himself as part of a revolutionary struggle to remake the world of stale conventions and unexamined authority.

The Scottish poet of peasant stock, Robert Burns (1759-96), offered a model of lyrical intensity and social idealism in a language that sounded fresh and spontaneous to his readers. Even Wordsworth who became more staid with age, exulted remembering the French Revolution:

> Bliss was it in that dawn to be alive,
> But to be young was very Heaven!

For much of the eighteenth century, the heroic couplet (iambic pentameter lines rhyming in pairs) was the dominant form of verse. In the period under consideration, poets experimented with many different forms in an attempt to find the form best suited to a variety of subjects and attitudes. Traditional ballads were collected; disused metres and stanza forms such as the Greek ode were revived; blank verse proved successful in meditative poems. In Shelley's long poem *Prometheus Unbound*, a variety of verse forms helps to alter the pace and the mood of the poem. Equally, an attempt was made to free the language of poetry from the dangers of a worn poetic diction and a register peculiar to one class of reader.

A note on the text

Eye-witness accounts survive describing Shelley's method of poetic composition. Ideas, images, phrases, rhythms occurred to him with great rapidity and he jotted them down in an almost illegible handwriting; later on he would return to his notebooks and redraft many times what he had originally scribbled down. 'The source of poetry', he said, 'is native and involuntary, but requires severe labor in its development.' Many of his poems were composed out of doors beside a stream, in the woods and even while lying in a small sailing boat. His punctuation, spelling, use of capitals and the various manuscript versions of the poems pose serious difficulties to the modern editor. His use of commas, dashes and semi-colons is different from twentieth-century usage and appears to have indicated the pace at which a poem should be read rather than the grammatical sense. Unexpected rhymes occur; for example, the end of 'pursuing' was apparently shortened to rhyme with 'ruin'. Furthermore, a number of the poems by which Shelley has become best known and sometimes criticised were left unfinished when he died, and some of his poems were published in England while he was in Italy and could not correct the printed version. Much of his prose and some of his most prized poems remained unpublished at his death.

His wife, Mary, edited and published *Posthumous Poems of Percy Bysshe Shelley* in 1824, and in 1839 she produced her edition of *The Poetical Works of Percy Bysshe Shelley* in four volumes. To this day, however, there is no complete and definitive text of either Shelley's poetry or his prose, although a great deal of progress has been made in the past few years. The texts of Shelley's poems considered in this book can be conveniently found in *Shelley: Selected Poems*, edited by Timothy Webb, Dent, London, 1977.

Part 2

Summaries
of SELECTED POEMS

'Mont Blanc'

Shelley wrote 'Mont Blanc' in July 1816 and it was published the following year. In the poem he explores the relationship between the human mind and external reality and speculates on the nature of the power which acts as the source of all order and thought. The opening section or verse paragraph presents an image of the mind as a course for the flow of perceived reality. In the second section this image is related to Shelley's present location, looking down into the ravine through which the river Arve rushes from its source amidst the glaciers high on the mountain. As he looks down on the noisy turmoil in the ravine, he is made aware (as in the opening image of the poem) of his own mind as a shaped and shaping instrument.

At the beginning of the third section Shelley muses on the possibility that the individual, conscious mind is fed from outside itself in a subconscious or barely conscious way, and in his speculation he sees Mont Blanc as a limit of the human mind. The absoluteness of the mountain peak provides a perspective on man's intellectual schemes; Shelley believes that through a contemplation of this absolute, men either arrive at a faith that they have a modest place in the world or have a scepticism forced upon them which clears away false ideas. Behind the transient happenings of nature and the schemes of men, Shelley sees an inaccessible and ultimately unknowable source of power, symbolised by Mont Blanc. Around this mystery, on the higher slopes of the mountain, are areas inhospitable to man, but, lower down, the glaciers give way to streams which give life to human settlements.

In the final section Shelley reiterates his vision of Mont Blanc as an inscrutable extremity but the poem ends with the suggestion, in the form of a question, that the human imagination can utilise even such unyielding material for its own designs.

COMMENTARY: At the same time as Shelley was writing the poem, he wrote in a letter to his friend Peacock:

> Mont Blanc was before us but was covered with cloud, and its base furrowed with dreadful gaps was seen alone. Pinnacles of snow, intolerably bright, part of the chain connected with Mont Blanc shone

through the clouds at intervals on high. I never knew, I never imagined what mountains were before. The immensity of these aerial summits excited, when they suddenly burst upon the sight, a sentiment of ecstatic wonder, not unallied to madness – And remember this was all one scene. It all pressed home to our regard and to our imagination. – Though it embraced a great number of miles the snowy pyramids which shot into the bright blue sky seemed to overhang our path – the ravine, clothed with gigantic pines and black with its depth below – so deep that the very roaring of the untameable Arve which rolled through it could not be heard above – was close to our very footsteps. All was as much our own as if we had been the creators of such impressions in the minds of others, as now occupied our own. – Nature was the poet whose harmony held our spirits more breathless than that of the divinest.

   . . . the ice of whose sides [the frozen waves of the glacier] is more beautifully azure than the sky. In these regions everything changes and is in motion. This vast mass of ice has one general progress which ceases neither day nor night. It breaks and rises forever; its undulations sink while others rise. From the precipices which surround it the echo of rocks which fall from their aerial summits, or of the ice and snow scarcely ceases for one moment. One would think that Mont Blanc was a living being and that the frozen blood forever circulated slowly through his stony veins.

The poem begins with an image of the mind and the beginning fixes the priorities; primarily, Shelley is not concerned with nature as such but with the way in which man understands the universe. The images of the river and the ravine are taken from what Shelley sees but he so introduces them that the mental process is given precedence; section 2, beginning, 'Thus thou, Ravine of Arve', moves out into external objects. Throughout the poem this interchange between the internal and the external takes place and both mental processes and the perceived world feed into 'the still cave of the witch Poesy' (line 44). Shelley repeatedly probes into such states as trance, sleep, death, fantasy because these mark the limits of our rational knowledge. The peak of Mont Blanc, whose appearance in the poem is dramatically held back until line 61, is the embodiment of a power indifferent to human aspirations or needs, 'Remote, serene and inaccessible' (line 97). Some commentators on Shelley interpret this power as Necessity (see p. 48); others see it as Permanence. In the context of Shelley's thought, Necessity seems more likely but he is not very specific in his description of the power. He is aware of some force underlying the happenings of the natural world, the geological shapes, the seasons, the destructiveness and the productiveness in nature, and he senses in mankind some presence of this power, both in man's general reasoning and in the individual's apprehension of reality. Shelley gives to imagination in the individual mind the strength to shape the discordant and elusive elements around it into acceptable patterns, but he asserts this point of view in the qualifying form of a rhetorical question at the end of the poem.

His belief in any kind of order is extremely precarious and the tentative quality of his thought is apparent in the labyrinthine syntax (re-read the opening eleven lines) and in the way elements in his mind bend back on themselves, fuse into each other and make categorical interpretation almost impossible. This sense of a flux, of something indefinite, is contributed to by the very long sentences in the first half of the poem, the mingling of abstract and concrete terms, images of darkness and light, noise and stillness, secrecy and knowledge, the shifts from the impersonal to the personal and, throughout, by the use of the blank verse, unconstrained by rhyme and with a rhythm so unobtrusive that we listen to the comings and goings of the poet's speculations.

NOTES AND GLOSSARY:

Mont Blanc: situated in Switzerland, the highest mountain in Europe, first climbed in 1786, and the subject of many poems (see, in particular, Coleridge's 'Hymn before Sun-rise in the Vale of Chamouni')

Vale of Chamouni: the valley of Chamonix in southeastern France through which the River Arve runs down into Lake Geneva. The River Rhône has its source in the lake

universe of things: all possible, perceivable objects and, Shelley would include, all thoughts related to such objects

tribute: contribution

its own: this seems to refer to the individual mind

assume: take on

awful: demanding awe

in likeness of: in the form of

gulfs: steep-sided bays

gird: surround (with a suggestion of guard)

brood: offspring

elder: former

aethereal: unsolid, more spiritual than material

unsculptured image: the rock behind the waterfall suggests a particular shape but the water preserves the possible image, suggestive but undefined

strange sleep: an enchantment of silence

lone: single, or sounding lonely

my own separate phantasy: his individual mind or imagination (but Shelley often suspected that the notion of an individual mind was an illusion)

unremitting interchange: unceasing giving and receiving

legion: multitude

that or thou: his individual mind or the ravine representing both a general human consciousness and the external world

unbidden: unwelcome

cave of the witch Poesy: creative imagination

Seeking: the subject of 'seeking' is 'my human mind' (line 37)

shadows . . . Ghosts . . . shade . . . phantom . . . image: Shelley is employing the idea expressed by Plato that the mind cannot apprehend the world of actuality directly but sees shadows cast by the real world on to the mind as on a screen

breast: the mysterious power which feeds all life and thought

they . . . thou: the shadows of reality . . . the actuality of the ravine as perceived in the imagination

remoter world: a superior dimension like Plato's realm of pure forms

death is slumber: birth and death, according to this view, are misconceptions: life is a part of a much larger existence

omnipotence: all-powerful force

unfurled: spread out (so that he cannot see)

inaccessibly: endlessly

homeless: unfixed

viewless: invisible

subject: lesser (as if they served a master)

unearthly: extraordinary, weird

deeps: depths of ice on the glacier

accumulated steeps: piled-up hills

Ghastly: causing horror

Earthquake-daemon: a spirit of nature who, when the earth was being shaped, experimented in creating wild, tormented shapes, a kind of decreation. In these lines Shelley refers to various theories about how the earth took its shape

mysterious: ambiguous, enigmatic

awful doubt: a scepticism about man's place in relation to the absoluteness of the wilderness

faith so mild . . . reconciled: a humble acceptance of man's position in the order of things. 'In' (line 79) is replaced by 'but' in many editions; both words occur in different manuscripts in Shelley's writing. 'In', however, makes easier and more consistent sense in the line

repeal . . . and woe: cancel or refute political and religious schemes of thought which present a false idea of man's place in the universe

the wise, the great, the good: Shelley may have had in mind the philosopher (who interprets), the artist (who causes others to feel) and the saint (who is specially sensitive)

daedal: wonderfully made (from Daedalus, the supreme craftsman in Greek mythology)

torpor: lethargy or inactivity (of winter)

detested trance: the hated suspension of winter

adverting: attentive, observant

Frost and sun: alternating cold and heat have caused the ice to form into extraordinary shapes

beaming: shining

retreat: hiding-place, place of security

smoke before . . . stream: smoke dispersed by the force of a storm

And their place is not known: no traces remain of man ('As for man, his days are as grass . . . For the wind passeth over it, and it is gone; and the place thereof shall know it no more.' Psalms 103:15–16)

circling: surrounding

Nor: neither

innocently: harmlessly

vapour: something unsubstantial

infinite dome/Of heaven: the entire universe

thee: Mont Blanc

And what were thou . . . vacancy?: if the human imagination could not create something out of 'silence and solitude', then the power apparent in Mont Blanc and all the large forces of the external world would be meaningless to man

---

'Ozymandias'

The poem was written late in 1817 and published early in 1818. Shelley exposes the vanity of tyranny and ambition and shows how time and the desert have no respect for the pretensions even of such a powerful ruler as Rameses II.

COMMENTARY: Shelley wrote his sonnet in competition with his friend Horace Smith. In terms of its rhyme scheme it is a very unconventional sonnet; punctuation and sense, however, preserve the common division between the octave (the first eight lines) and the sestet (the final six lines). Shelley detaches the thought of the poem from himself by presenting the description as the words of a traveller and, although he had almost certainly read detailed accounts of the statue in the ruined city of Thebes, beside the Nile, he deliberately sets the statue in isolation in the desert. The enormous size of the dismembered figure emphasises the vanity of Rameses; the legs standing on their own look ridiculous, the body seems to have disappeared and the face of the Pharaoh is reduced to a series of expressions. The arrogant inscription (lines 10–11) now reads as an ironic comment on the proud Pharaoh and Shelley completes the image of futility with his description of the empty desert around the ruin. 'Look on my works', the inscription commands, but 'Nothing beside remains' to be seen.

The sonnet form and particularly its more usual rhyme schemes can be very constricting, but Shelley succeeds in writing a sonnet which sounds unforced and even conversational. The unusual rhyme scheme he adopts allows him to control his thought but not in an obtrusively obvious manner. He is prepared to use half-rhyme in lines 2 and 4, and 9 and 11, and throughout the poem the syntax and punctuation units are varied to interplay with the rhyme scheme and the regular length of the lines. Small variations in the basic iambic stress pattern help to avoid monotony. The octave is connected to the sestet by the rhyming words 'things' and 'kings' in lines 7 and 10 and the cool statement of the final three lines is emphasised by the repetition of the rhyming vowel which gathers together 'remains', 'decay', 'bare', 'away' and links them with 'despair' in line 11.

NOTES AND GLOSSARY:

Ozymandias:	the Greek name of Rameses II (1304–1237BC) who, according to the biblical scholars of Shelley's time, was the pharaoh of Egypt who oppressed the captive Hebrews and opposed the wishes of Moses to free them. He had many huge buildings and monuments constructed in his own honour
traveller:	Shelley may have met someone who had visited Egypt but it is more probable that he had read about the statue in a book such as Richard Pococke's *A Description of the East and Some Other Countries* (1743)
antique:	with an ancient history
trunkless:	without a body
visage:	face
wrinkled lip:	his lip curled in contempt or disdain
cold:	arrogant, unfeeling
read:	understood
yet survive:	outlive (the 'hand' and 'heart' of the following line)
stamped:	depicted, carved

lifeless things:	stones
hand:	the sculptor
mocked them:	imitated, showed artistically the passions of Ozymandias; or showed the passions as contemptible
heart that fed:	the heart of Ozymandias which encouraged such passions
My name ... and despair:	Diodorus Siculus, a Greek historian of the first century BC, quotes an inscription on a huge statue in Egypt: 'I am Ozymandias, king of kings; if anyone wishes to know how great I am and where I lie, let him surpass any of my works.'
colossal:	huge (originally used by the Greeks to describe the huge statues of Ancient Egypt)

'The Mask of Anarchy'

Shelley wrote the poem in September 1819 and sent it to his friend Leigh Hunt for immediate publication in the newspaper, the *Examiner*, but it remained unpublished until 1832. Incensed at the reports of the Massacre at Manchester (see below), Shelley intended his poem to stir the people of England to a passive resistance against the forces of oppression.

The poem takes the form of a vision in which Shelley sees a procession of allegorical figures subservient to Anarchy, the centre of corrupt and cruel power. Anarchy rides through England trampling to death the crowds of his admirers and, with his helpers, terrorising the people. He is presented by Shelley as a figure of death but his supporters, shown as lawyers and priests, see him as holy and expect to be rewarded for their obedience. Their triumphal procession to occupy the centres of power in London is interrupted by the arrival of Hope, in the shape of a dishevelled girl, who feels so despondent at the oppression having gone on for so long that she lies down on the road and waits to be trampled. She is saved from death by the sudden intervention of a Shape, representing the enlightened mind: Anarchy is immediately and miraculously destroyed and his horse tramples his murderous supporters as it flees.

The remainder of the poem consists of the words which emanate from the Shape, words which seem like the expression of nature or of England itself. The English are rebuked for having accepted their loss of liberty and basic rights as something inevitable; they have given their labour for the benefit of their masters, and, when they have noticed the unfairness of this system, they have been filled with useless wishes for revenge. Even wild animals and primitive man have experienced better lives. Freedom is not some fantasy but consists of actual conditions which allow men to live decently and rationally with one another. The Shape urges Englishmen to unite to form a Parliament which can assert the values of freedom with such strength that tyrants and ambitious men cannot break the will of the people. The old common law of England is on their side and if they meet force with stoicism and non-violent resolution, cruelty and hatred will be defeated.

COMMENTARY: In 1819 Shelley wrote the bulk of his long masterpiece, the lyrical drama *Prometheus Unbound*, and a tragedy, *The Cenci*. Although by now resident in Italy and with no strong inclination to return to Britain, he kept himself well informed about British politics by having newspapers sent out to him and by maintaining a correspondence with friends in Britain. For most of Shelley's life until the eventual defeat of Napoleon at Waterloo in 1815, Britain had been at war with France. In the years after the end of the war, Britain was in a precarious state. Vast numbers of demobilised soldiers and sailors added to the problem of grave unemployment, money declined in buying power, and food was scarce because of a series of disastrous harvests and laws which forbade the importation of foreign food-stuffs; the government was nervousIy helpless to rectify the economic situation and saw repression as the only feasible response to a turmoil which might lead to revolution. At a time when a city such as Birmingham with a population of over seventy thousand had no Member of Parliament and employers had absolute power over their workers, the two crucial issues concerned parliamentary representation and the right of working people to associate in trade unions. A gathering of possibly eighty thousand people in St Peter's Fields, Manchester were listening to Henry 'Orator' Hunt talking on these issues when an attempt was made by the authorities to arrest him. In the struggle which followed, a troop of regular cavalry charged into the crowd, killing about a dozen and wounding about five hundred.

In order to try to communicate with a wide audience, Shelley wrote his poem in a rough, four- or five-line ballad stanza, familiar to many from popular songs. Allowing for many impure rhymes, the rhyme scheme is consistent; the majority of the lines, however, are not end-stopped (that is, the sense runs on without punctuation) and quite a number of stanzas run on into the following one, adding to the speed of the poem and saving the verse from becoming too mechanical. Although the stress pattern is irregular, the three or four stresses in each line have a heavy tread which contributes to a crude, ingenuous quality in the poetry. The images, too, have a cartoon flavour and the extravagant, surreal description of the characters keeps reminding the reader that this is not a realistic account of the Peterloo Massacre but a vision of what might happen.

Shelley's vision is in two parts. Lines 5–146 describe the 'ghastly masquerade'; lines 147–376 are the words of the Shape. In his letter to Hunt accompanying the poem, he wrote:

> I fear that in England things will be carried violently by the rulers, and that they will not have learned to yield in time to the spirit of the age. The great thing to do is to hold the balance between popular impatience and tyrannical obstinacy; to inculcate with fervour both the right of resistance and the duty of forbearance.

The figure of Hope, introduced in line 86, has become so despondent at the apparent omnipotence of Anarchy that she is resigned to die. It is to save Hope that the Shape intervenes. Without hope, reform and progress are impossible, but hope is insufficient in itself to effect a change from the prevailing corrupt power. In order that the true revolution can take place – and Shelley was remembering the mistakes in the French Revolution – men must recognise their present condition of slavery, economic and psychological, and envisage a situation of freedom. Through the voice of the Shape, Shelley stresses, as he does elsewhere in his writings, knowledge and imagination as the bases for humane development, and he emphasises the need for a continuity between the wisdom acquired in older times and the direction of contemporary change.

The strongest aspects of the poem are the caricature descriptions of Government ministers at the beginning and Shelley's diagnosis of subservience and liberty in the second half. The main weakness in the thought of the poem is not in Shelley's faith in the potential political power of passive disobedience; granted certain conditions, it might succeed. The central weakness stems from the vagueness with which the Shape is described and the obscure miracle by which the Shape destroys Anarchy and saves Hope. Is this destruction an example of passive resistance? Shelley, it is evident in many of his writings, wanted to believe that a bloodless revolution was possible but he had serious doubts about its feasibility and chances of success, and this unresolved problem flaws the middle of the poem.

NOTES AND GLOSSARY:

The Mask of Anarchy: Shelley wishes to suggest both the disguise worn by the forces of misrule and the masque or pageant described in the first part of the poem

the Massacre at Manchester: see Commentary above

Castlereagh: Foreign Secretary (1812–22) and leader of the Tory Party in the House of Commons. He had been ruthless in suppressing troubles in Ireland and was antipathetic to the Revolutionary movement in France

seven bloodhounds: at the Congress of Vienna in 1815, seven European countries with Britain agreed not to press for the immediate abolition of the slave-trade; the 'human hearts' (line 12) are presumably slaves

plight: condition

Eldon: the Lord Chancellor (shown by his 'ermined gown'), famous not only for his harsh judgments but also for bursting into tears in court. After his first wife Harriet died, Shelley lost custody of their children because of a ruling by Eldon

Sidmouth: the Home Secretary responsible for many repressive measures. He used agents to provoke trouble in order to expose the more militant workers, who were then deported or hanged. A million pounds of government money was spent at his suggestion in building churches in the poorest areas of cities; Christianity would, he felt, encourage people to accept suffering passively

Anarchy: Shelley believed that bad government breeds chaos and violence; despotism is a denial of good order. In the Bible (Revelation 6:8) the fourth of the Riders of the Apocalypse is described: 'And I looked, and behold a pale horse: and his name that sat on him was Death, and Hell followed with him. And power was given unto them over the fourth part of the earth, to kill with sword, and with hunger, and with death, and with the beasts of the earth.'

wine of desolation: the perverted pleasure in destruction

sceptre . . . gold-inwoven robe: emblems of kingship

Bank: the Bank of England, centre of the country's wealth

Tower: the Tower of London, where the Crown Jewels are kept

pensioned: corrupt, bought

Maniac: driven mad

My father time: ordinary people through history

palsied: paralysed

vapour of a vale: mist in a valley

Shape: this indefinite figure has been interpreted as liberty, enlightenment, nature, England, the people. Shelley chooses not to be too specific

arrayed in mail: clothed in armour (suggesting a warrior)

viper's scale: snake-skin (Shelley does not always use snakes as symbolic of evil)

grain: texture or pattern

planet, like the Morning's: Venus, the planet of Love

mien: expression

accent unwithstood: unresisted or irresistible utterance

Heroes of unwritten story: ordinary people not mentioned in history books

Nurslings ... Mother: all nurtured by Nature

slumber: the sleep of subservience

pine and peak: waste away

riot: extravagance

surfeiting: suffering from over-eating

Ghost of Gold: paper money

its substance: real gold

forgery/Of the title deeds: paper money, because it can be printed and its value manipulated by governments, gives no assurance to the people who work to produce goods and allows them to be used by the manipulators

Birds find rest: the following twelve lines echo the verse in the Bible where Jesus says: 'The foxes have holes, and the birds of the air have nests; but the Son of man hath not where to lay his head.' (Matthew 8:20)

living graves: people in slavery are half alive and half dead

demand: question

imposters: false, pessimistic or reactionary political thinkers

cave of Fame: rumour or idle speculation

check: moderating factor

snake: when threatened, the snake can bite

Priests make such ado: Shelley believed that the promise of heaven and the threat of hell only made sense to people who were not sufficiently freed from want and oppression to be able to think clearly

Leagued ... in Gaul: in 1793 the countries around France, including Britain, united to crush the revolution there

the rich have kissed: Jesus advised the rich man, 'Sell all that thou hast, and distribute unto the poor, and thou shalt have treasure in heaven: and come, follow me.' (Luke 18:22). Shelley had inherited considerable wealth but was very generous with it

Drew the power ... prey: the enlightened rich fight against the very evils which made them rich

cot: cottage

workhouse: an institution paid for by the government where poor and unemployed people could work in exchange for some food and shelter. The system was harsh and allowed brutal exploitation to take place

tares:	weeds or unprofitable habits
prison-halls of wealth and fashion:	the rich and sophisticated are not free; they are locked in their own habits of thought
targes:	shields
shade:	protection
emblazonry:	colourful display
scimitars:	swords with curved blades
sphereless:	like falling stars
phalanx:	closely packed, heavily defensive military formation
Arbiters:	judges, those who decide
old laws of England:	traditional notions of rights and fairness which have developed from the time of Alfred the Great (AD849–99)
heralds:	the individuals who have advanced these laws (see preceding note)
true warriors:	Shelley appears to accept that some wars may be necessary but he rejects the kind of class warfare that was seen at Peterloo
oracular:	wise and prophetic
volcano:	suggesting an irrepressible force which must be released

'England in 1819'

The poem was written late in 1819 but was not published until 1839. Shelley describes the condition of England under George III and hopes that change will come.

COMMENTARY: In 1819 and 1820, Shelley had the idea of publishing a book of political poems. Although the book was never published, he did write a number of poems which can be read together. These poems reflect his anger at the political situation of the time and his idealism that a new sanity and justice can replace the violence and corruption. Mary Shelley, in her Note to the poems of 1819, writes: 'He believed that a clash between the two classes of society was inevitable, and he eagerly ranged himself on the people's side.'

This sonnet is formally unusual in two respects. The division marked by the rhyme scheme comes after the sixth line, not, as is more common, after the eighth; and Shelley uses only four rhyme sounds, thereby giving a very condensed quality to the sonnet. Each line moves with heavy deliberation contributing to a prosecution case completed by the dash after line 12 and suddenly knocked down or, at least, brought into question by the final opposing couplet of lines 13 and 14. From the opening line with its six pronounced stresses, the first twelve lines operate as a series of categorical statements emphasising Shelley's contempt first for the oppressors and then for the institutions and instruments of oppression. Alliteration, regularity of stress and the images of depravity and blood contribute to the force of Shelley's accusation. Dramatically, with its accumulation of condemnations and the surprising release, the poem is very effective but, although Shelley qualifies any easy optimism with the conditional 'may' (line 13), the 'glorious Phantom' is rather insubstantial to perform the task asked of it.

NOTES AND GLOSSARY:

King: George III had reigned since 1760 and was to die in 1820 at the age of eighty-one. He had suffered from bouts of madness for many years and in 1811 was declared insane

Princes: George III had nine sons and they were notorious for their debauched living. Shelley probably refers particularly to the Prince Regent who ruled for his father from 1811 and eventually became King as George IV in 1820. His conduct was disgusting

dull race: the house of Hanover, their family

leechlike: a leech is a worm with a sucker by which it attaches itself to its victim while it sucks blood, a clinging parasite. It drops off when it has sucked its fill

drop . . . a blow: when they are filled (as if blind drunk) with what others need, they leave the victim who is so weakened that he cannot protect himself

people . . . field: see notes on the Peterloo Massacre in the Commentary on 'The Mask of Anarchy'

liberticide: destroying of liberty

prey: victim of oppression

two-edged sword: one that can cut in two directions. Shelley suggests that the soldiers can become so disgusted that they may turn on their rulers

Golden . . . and slay: a legal system based on wealth and power forces poor people into crime and then punishes them

Religion: the form of religion, a set of inhibiting rules, which has no connection with the teachings of Christ in the Bible

Senate: parliament is opposed to what it should be: it needs to be reformed

Are graves: all the preceding evils are dead and, Shelley hopes, can be buried in the past

Phantom: the spirit of the new age, revolution, enlightenment, freedom are possible interpretations (see note on the Shape in 'The Mask of Anarchy')

| may: | Shelley hopes; he does not say it 'will' burst |
| illumine ... day: | bring light after the darkness and peace after the violence |

'Ode to the West Wind'

The poem was written in the autumn of 1819 and published in the volume containing *Prometheus Unbound* in 1820. Shelley is concerned with the regeneration of himself poetically and spiritually and of Europe politically. The west wind is seen as the force necessary to effect this regeneration. In the first three stanzas aspects of nature through the seasons, on land, in the air and in the sea, demonstrate the different moods and powers of the wind, and Shelley addresses the wind personally as if it were a deity. In the fourth stanza, Shelley likens himself to the leaf, the cloud and the wave, subject to the force of the wind, but recognises that age and experience have deprived him of the freedom and hope he had felt when he was younger. Finally, he appeals to the wind, the wind of inspiration and change, to reinvigorate him and to give force and persuasiveness to his poetry of revolution.

COMMENTARY: Composed between 'The Mask of Anarchy' and 'England in 1819', this ode reflects a similar mixture of depression and optimism to that found in these two poems; here, however, Shelley presents his emotions with a more personal flavour and finds his imagery, not in public events, but in the forces of nature. The final part of *Prometheus Unbound* which he was completing at this time makes a similar use of natural imagery, but the particular attention given to autumn, spring and the wind looks back to a passage in *The Revolt of Islam*, Canto IX, stanzas xxi–xxx.

In a note Shelley describes the immediate situation in which he wrote the poem:

This poem was conceived and chiefly written in a wood that skirts the Arno, near Florence, and on a day when that tempestuous wind, whose temperature is at once mild and animating, was collecting the vapours which pour down the autumnal rains. They began, as I foresaw, at sunset with a violent tempest of hail and rain, attended by that magnificent thunder and lightning peculiar to the Cisalpine regions.

Formally, the poem consists of five stanzas, each a sonnet formed of four units of terza rima completed by a couplet. In terza rima, the verse form so brilliantly handled in *The Divine Comedy* by the Italian poet, Dante (1265–1321), the first and third lines rhyme and the rhyme sound of the second line is taken up by the fourth and sixth lines. This linked chain gives a feeling of onward movement; the reader is driven forward in anticipation of the completion of the rhyme. Commonly, the sense surges on past the end of the line and the verse has a breathless quality in keeping with the description of the wind's movement. The lines generally have five stresses, the stress tending to fall on the even syllables, but many of the lines are made to sound arresting by opening with a stressed syllable. This sense of dramatic directness fits with the intense address of the poet to the wind in the repeated 'Thou'.

The first three stanzas end with the invocation, 'O hear!' and the whole poem takes the form of a prayer. As is common in prayers, the first half of the poem describes the attributes, both frightening and consoling, of the deity. The powers of the west wind are manifested through the seasons of the year as a destroyer, preserver and creator, and in the elements of nature on land, in the air and in the sea. Up until the fourth stanza there is no mention of the supplicant, but in the final two stanzas the poet confesses his own frailties and implores the deity to make the poet's work part of a spiritual awakening of a new year. Although only twenty-seven years old, Shelley feels jaded and disappointed; his work has not received the attention for which he hoped and around him in Europe he sees little cause for optimism. In this mood of inadequacy, Shelley acknowledges his need for a force beyond his own calculation to lift him and to disseminate a new gospel of hope.

The composition is given a subtle, unified texture by the overlapping of images, the echo of words, rhyme sounds and alliterative patterns, and the frequent similes; yet, throughout the poem, Shelley modulates the language in accord with the changing aspects of the wind and his musings on it and on himself. Always the divine nature of the wind is stressed. In the opening stanza the autumn wind is a sinister 'enchanter' and charioteer of dead bodies before the spring wind is presented as an idyllic shepherdess and summoner of life (with her clarion); the ghosts and dark and cold are contrasted with the azure and sweet and living. The second stanza, with the onset of the winter storms, produces images of violence, destruction and possession. The wind disrupts the usual order, in a 'commotion' with 'tangled boughs of Heaven and Ocean' and the demonic figure of the Maenad (see notes below) is threatening. The 'dirge' and 'vast sepulchre' of this stanza are replaced in the third stanza by the images of clear water, light, balmy winds and a state of trance. By the end of the third stanza, however, the note of fear and menace has returned. In the final stanzas, Shelley weaves into the verse many of these earlier images but now set in a more personal context of his childhood and present dejection, before he broadens out to the 'universe', 'mankind' and 'Earth'. The admiration for the power of the wind and the urgency of Shelley's plea rise to a crescendo in the final stanza with the strong verbs 'drive' and 'scatter' (reminiscent of the beginning of the poem) and the cry for identification with the wind, 'Be thou, Spirit fierce,/My spirit! Be thou me' and 'Be through my lips . . . .The trumpet of a prophecy!'

The very end of the poem is perplexing. We expect another rhapsodic exclamation but the poem closes with a question. Shelley is not quite so certain as his build-up suggested and at the final moment a doubt vexes his mind. Can regeneration arrive so mechanically?

NOTES AND GLOSSARY:

Ode to the West Wind: The word 'ode' in Greek means a song. In Ancient Greek poetry, the Choral or Pindaric Ode was written in a particular form and was intended to be sung. By Shelley's time, an Ode had come to mean a fairly short poem of a meditative, lyrical sort often written in a complicated verse form and often addressing an abstract quality or aspect of Nature in a personal way.

The west wind is the prevailing wind for much of the year in Western Europe and, because it comes in from the Atlantic, it tends to be mild. In the autumn, however, the west wind can be very violent. Shelley uses capital letters to give a superior status to the wind. In the Indo-European languages there is a strong connection between words for wind, spirit, inspiration, breath and soul

enchanter: worker of magic. 'Enchant' originally meant to sing a spell and is the same word as 'incant'. Compare the 'incantation of this verse' in the final stanza

Yellow . . . red: the colours of decaying leaves. It has been pointed out that these are the colours of the different races of human beings

hectic: fevered (the high colour associated with wasting diseases)

Pestilence: extremely infectious disease of the sort which destroyed whole communities and caused terror until modern times

chariotest: carry or steer (with the suggestion of a solemn transporting to the underworld)

winged seeds: many plants, including trees, perpetuate themselves by seeds borne on the wind

like a corpse: not really dead but in suspended animation in the earth

azure: clear blue (of the cloudless sky)

Sister: a different, gentler, more maternal aspect of the west wind

clarion: trumpet used to arouse or summon

like flocks: as if the new buds are being shepherded to pastures after the winter

living hues: vivid colours (after the drabness of winter)

moving: not just present but actively working in everything

Destroyer and Preserver: in Hindu mythology, the three principal deities are Siva the Destroyer, Brahma the Creator, and Vishnu the Preserver (whose name means the one who works everywhere)

stream: flow of the wind

steep: high (suggesting the abrupt and spacious movements of cloud and air)

shed: scattered, shaken off

tangled ... Ocean: clouds created by the evaporation from the sea are partly air and partly water. Shelley may be referring to the water-spouts which he had certainly seen in this area and which he described as 'black trunks'. The 'boughs' continues the general image of trees and leaves from stanza one

Angels: messengers, heralds

bright hair ... Maenad: a Maenad was a female devotee of Dionysus, the Greek god of wine, revelry and vegetation. The worshipping Maenads appeared to be possessed by the god's power and acted as if mad. Shelley describes her hair as streaming out from her head and, in comparing the clouds in the rising wind to the Maenad, he is suggesting the demonic power of the storm

dim verge: the sky at the horizon is dark with storm clouds

zenith: highest point in the sky

locks: strands of hair. The cloud formation called cirrus is derived from the Latin word for curls

dirge: song of mourning for a dead person

closing night: the clouds are thickening and darkness is coming on

Vaulted: forming a curved roof

congregated ... vapours: the clouds are now so dense that the sky appears solid. The power of the wind is concentrated to an ultimate pressure before the storm explodes

Lulled ... streams: soothed, almost hypnotised, by the slow turning of the clear currents in the water

pumice: porous stone made from volcanic lava

Baiae's bay: west of Naples in Southern Italy, in a notoriously volcanic area

in sleep: unmoving and locked as if in a dream

old palaces and towers: in Roman times, emperors had built palaces in the bay. As a resort it was notorious for its luxury and immorality. An alteration in the sea level covered the town with water but the buildings still stand and Shelley had himself seen them the previous year. He would have considered them as symbols of aristocratic and corrupt power

intenser: magnifying because of the combination of strong sunlight and clear water

azure ... flowers: the weeds growing underwater are given a magical quality by the water and sunlight

sense ... them: the eye loses its focus because the image in the water keeps subtly changing

Atlantic: possibly Shelley had in mind the revolution which had taken place in America and whose effects could be felt in Europe

level powers: flat waves

Cleave ... chasms: break into deep waves

oozy woods: the tall slimy seaweeds growing on the seabed

know ... themselves: Shelley writes in a note: 'The phenomenon alluded to at the conclusion of the third stanza is well known to naturalists. The vegetation at the bottom of the sea, of rivers, and of lakes, sympathizes with that of the land in the change of seasons, and is consequently influenced by the winds which announce it.' The old order of the Roman emperors, complacent in its easy power, had to accept the intimation of its destruction

despoil: tear off their leaves (in fear). Notice how the leaf image is used in all three opening stanzas

my boyhood ... vision: Shelley may be speaking metaphorically about his younger, idealistic days, but the image of rivalling the wind probably comes from memories of chasing the moving shadow on the earth of the flying clouds above

striven ... sore need: the wind is the power of inspiration (among other things) and Shelley remembers times when he felt inspired

I fall ... I bleed: Shelley concedes that he feels defeated by the misfortunes and pains he has experienced. It is because he is so dejected and absorbed in his misery that he needs the restoring power of the wind

weight of hours: time, dull habit

tameless . . . proud: he had these qualities once but he has lost them

lyre: the aeolian harp was placed on a hillside and made musical sounds as the wind blew through it. Shelley discusses this image of the poet and inspiration at the beginning of his 'Defence of Poetry'

my leaves: his hair is growing thin

both: Shelley ('thy lyre') and the forest

dead thoughts: previously written but unsuccessful poems

quicken: stimulate or give life to, or speed up

incantation: ritual recitation (with the suggestion of a magic charm)

unextinguished hearth: fire which is still alive (the negative suggests an obstinate defiance)

my words: he may have had in mind his visionary poem about man's condition, *Prometheus Unbound*

through my lips: Shelley is simply a vehicle or medium through which inspiration or revelation is uttered

unawakened: like the earth in winter in stanza one (line 10), the world of men is asleep and ignorant of future possibilities

trumpet of a prophecy: announcement of a new era. Shelley may intend an echo of the trumpet in the Bible, which signals the beginning of Christ's rule on earth (Revelation 9)

'To a Skylark'

The poem was written in June 1820 near Livorno in Italy and published later that year in a volume with *Prometheus Unbound*. There are three main parts in the thought of the poem. Lines 1–30 describe the poet's experience of the bird as a barely seen, imagined and sharply felt phenomenon. In the second part, lines 31–60, Shelley attempts to identify the essential nature of the bird by describing analogous happenings. From line 61 to the end, he relates the song of the skylark and what that song consists of to the aspirations and situation of human beings, and asks the spirit-bird so to instruct him as a poet that the world would come to an understanding of the mystery represented by the bird.

COMMENTARY: 'It was on a beautiful summer evening,' Mary Shelley writes in a note, 'while wandering among the lanes whose myrtle-hedges were the bowers of the fire-flies, that we heard the carolling of the skylark which inspired one of the most beautiful of his poems.' In the months prior to this Shelley had been re-reading Plato and his speculations on the nature of the soul. Plato writes of the soul in *Phaedrus*:

When it is perfect and fully winged it soars in the upper air and orders the entire universe; but the soul that has lost its feathers sinks down till it finds some solid resting place. The wing is the bodily part most related to the divine . . . . Now of that divine region no earthly poet has ever sung, or ever will sing in a manner worthy of it . . . but I must venture to express the truth.

These two quotations from Mary Shelley and Plato indicate that Shelley is concerned in the poem both with the actual beauty of the bird's song and with the divine essence, the aspiration of the soul and the force of inspiration symbolised by the bird.

The stanza form with its four short lines and one final longer line and only two rhyme sounds is very subtly used, sometimes suggesting the soaring and floating flight of the skylark, sometimes suggesting the song of the bird being reeled out and in. The final, longer line often acts as a statement giving a sense of considered completion to the stanzas which operate as single sentences.

In the first third of the poem, Shelley tries to grasp the experience (hearing the bird) which is at the extreme edge of his mind: 'We hardly see – we feel that it is there.' Even in this part, he is forced to write in similes and parallels; the bird and what it represents cannot be apprehended directly. Lines 31 and 32 concede this difficulty and the following section offers a series of earthly situations which share something of his experience of the bird. Each of the four similes in lines 36–55 presents a hidden source of some beauty which spills into the surrounding world, and Shelley's vision of the skylark is enriched by association with different but related manifestations of beauty. What, Shelley goes on to enquire, can be the source, the inspiration of such superhuman beauty? Obviously, human beings, even poets, are so tied to the earth, to hopes and regrets, that they cannot rival the pure quality found in the bird. It is possible, however, that the poet can learn from the example of the bird and can be so inspired that, just as he marvels at something beyond himself, so the reader would be moved by a poetic vision normally beyond his own capability. This poem itself constitutes an example of what Shelley aspires to, and the mixture of imagery of the ethereal and the beautiful earthly elements conveys, as does the very idea of the skylark, a sense of an elevated dimension at the extreme frontier of human understanding.

NOTES AND GLOSSARY:

skylark:	a small bird which flies very steeply into the sky. It sings while in flight and is often at a height where it cannot be seen but only heard
Heaven:	the highest point of the sky but also Plato's realm of ideal forms (see p. 7)

profuse strains:	lavish songs
unpremeditated:	spontaneous
cloud of fire:	lit up by the low sun of evening
race:	rush, impetus
pale . . . flight:	the soft colour of the evening sky becomes lighter away from the actual body of the bird
star of Heaven:	the star is invisible in daylight but it is still there in the sky
silver sphere:	Venus, the bright morning star, whose light ('arrows') seems sharpest just before it disappears in daylight
bare:	with no other clouds
unbidden:	not according to anyone's command and probably not even obeying his own will
bower:	the word is used for both a bedroom in a castle and a shaded sitting place in a garden
dell:	small hollow
unbeholden:	from a hidden place; or without obligation to anyone (compare 'unbidden')
aerial:	light and delicate
embowered:	enclosed
deflowered:	assaulted and robbed
thieves:	the winds, or possibly bees
vernal:	spring, fresh
rapture:	passionate excitement
Hymeneal:	celebrating marriage
triumphal:	celebrating victory
vaunt:	boast
want:	lack
joyance:	feeling or state of gladness
languor:	weariness
satiety:	tired distaste (as if after over-indulging in food or drink)
deem:	judge, consider
pine:	waste away with longing
fraught:	filled, troubled
skill to poet were:	as an example or inspiration
scorner:	the skylark sings only when flying and is more a creature of the sky than of the earth
harmonious madness:	a very Platonic idea. Shelley's translation of Plato's *Ion* reads: 'The Muse, communicating through those whom she has first inspired, to all others capable of sharing in the inspiration, the influence of that first enthusiasm, creates a chain

and a succession. For the authors of those great poems which we admire, do not attain to excellence through the rules of any art, but they utter their beautiful melodies of verse in a state of inspiration, and, as it were, possessed of a spirit not their own . . . in a state of divine insanity.'

Adonais

Written between April and June 1821, the poem was published in July of the same year. The first eight stanzas are mainly addressed to Urania, the mother of Adonais, who was not present when he died and who must now accept that he has passed into the kingdom of death. In stanzas 9–17 a procession of mourners representing aspects of his poetic creation, nature and England, come to tend his dead body and lament his loss. How absolute the death of Adonais appears is emphasised by the contrast drawn in stanzas 18–21 between winter which with all its bleakness, gives way to spring and rebirth, and the stark, ungiving deadness of Adonais. Urania travels from her home to utter her lamentation over her son's body and to condemn the cruel forces responsible for his killing (stanzas 22–9). She is joined by a group of his fellow shepherd-poets who are described in stanzas 30–7, and they join with Urania in rebuking the oppressors of Adonais. In stanza 38 a reversal begins in which the corporeal death of Adonais is accepted while his spiritual survival is asserted. He is now seen as being reunited with nature and as an addition to the beauty and achievement of the world; as such he is immortal. In stanzas 47–51 the mourner is commanded to compare the happy fate of Adonais with his own miserable situation in life, and the poem reaches its climax in a call for the reader to join himself to this superior reality; Shelley makes it clear, however, that such an enterprise is hazardous and requires courage.

COMMENTARY: John Keats, aged twenty-five, died of tuberculosis in Rome on 23 February 1821. Shelley, who had earlier invited Keats to stay with him in Italy, heard news of Keats's death early in April and believed that hostile reviews of Keats's poem *Endymion* in 1818 had aggravated his illness and hastened his end. In Shelley's mind, Keats represented young poetic genius persecuted and martyred by a literary and social establishment and, in this, he saw a similarity between Keats and himself. Immediately prior to his work on *Adonais*, Shelley had written his 'Defence of Poetry' 'in honour of my mistress Urania'; the two works operate together to promote the crucial function, as Shelley sees it, of the poet in a hostile or indifferent world. The ungenerosity of literary critics to new talent, is, he alleges, symptomatic of a lack of appreciation throughout society of beauty and truth.

Keats's death was the particular instigation of *Adonais* but the poem does not seek to offer a biographical account of Keats. Nor does it aim to sound like a personal lament by Shelley; he appears as 'I' really only in the first line and at the very end. The poem is a pastoral elegy based on models which date back to the Greek Sicilian poets, Theocritus (third century BC), Bion and Moschus (second century BC). Shelley translated part of the 'Elegy on the Death of Adonis' attributed to Bion and part of the 'Elegy on the Death of Bion' attributed to Moschus. He was familiar, also, with the two most famous examples in English: *Astrophel* by Edmund Spenser (1552-99), on the death of the poet Sir Philip Sidney; and *Lycidas* by John Milton (1609-74), on the death of a student contemporary, Edward King. The features of *Adonais* described in the summary above are characteristics of the pastoral elegy: the absence of the protector at the moment of death, the natural (pastoral) setting with the main figures seen as shepherds, the lament of nature, the procession of mourners, the transformation of the dead person into something eternal and of grief into rejoicing.

The point of the pastoral elegy is not to express personal grief but to attempt a justification of human suffering and death. The first thirty-seven stanzas of Shelley's poem are more obviously related to the conventions of the pastoral elegy and to the myth of Adonis (see note on Adonais below), but the final part after the pivotal stanza 38 develops many thoughts and images from the earlier part. Shelley proclaims a new perspective according to which death is not a separation from nature; the true fame of poetic immortality is contrasted with the previous worldly reputation established by false critics, and a notion of truth is pointed to which is inaccessible to men caught in time and earthly concerns. In his 'Defence of Poetry', Shelley writes of 'that great poem, which all poets, like the co-operating thoughts of one great mind, have built up since the beginning of the world' and that great poem, to which Adonais-Keats has contributed, is the beacon Shelley sees through the disappointments and dark brutalities of ordinary life.

The way in which Shelley fuses contemporary events, particularly related to Keats, and mythical elements, particularly related to the story of Adonis, is not unique and can be compared with Milton's method in *Lycidas* and that of T. S. Eliot (1888-1965) in *The Waste Land*. The density of reference and the capacity of the poem to support different levels of interpretation are essential aspects of what Shelley himself described as 'a highly wrought piece of art', and they help to give resonance and a universal significance to the personal and contemporary. Running through the poem and giving it unity and indicating the shifts in thought, there are patterns of imagery, the main ones relating to nature, particularly the seasonal changes, animals, light and darkness. As is common in Shelley, however, the imagery is not tied tightly to the concrete; it lifts from the actual world of sensations towards the abstract and the intellectual.

The Spenserian stanza used in *Adonais* originated in Edmund Spenser's *The Faerie Queene* at the end of the sixteenth century. Keats used it in *The Eve of St Agnes* and Shelley employed it in *The Revolt of Islam*. In each stanza, the first eight lines, basically iambic pentameters, rhyme *a b a b b c b c*, with the fourth and fifth lines sharing a rhyme sound so that the two quatrains are held together. The final line has an extra stress and, in being longer and rhyming with the previous line, it has the effect of rounding off the sense and sound of the stanza.

NOTES AND GLOSSARY:

Adonais: in Greek mythology, Adonis is a handsome youth who is loved by Aphrodite, the goddess of love. While she is absent he is killed by a wild boar during a hunt. Aphrodite pleads with the gods of the underworld that Adonis be released from death. According to the myth he is allowed to live in the world for half the year. Adonis thus comes to be associated with the cycle of the seasons and he was worshipped as a god of fertility who is resurrected each spring. The name Adonai in Hebrew means lord and Shelley does not wish to stick to one single meaning of the name. The name is pronounced with four syllables

Epigraph: Shelley translated these lines in Greek attributed to Plato: 'Thou wert the morning star among the living/Ere thy fair light had fled;-/Now, having died thou art as Hesperus, giving/New splendour to the dead.' The planet Venus appears both as the morning star (Lucifer) and as the evening star (Hesperus)

sad Hour: Shelley personifies the moment in time as if it is responsible for what happens

obscure compeers: all other moments of time

mighty Mother: Aphrodite had two aspects: Pandemos of physical love and Urania of spiritual love. Shelley chooses to use a mother figure of spiritual love, Urania, as appropriate to Adonais (Keats) rather than the lover of the Adonis story. Urania was also the Muse of astronomy and came to represent (in Milton, for example) the Muse, or inspiration, of the highest poetry

shaft ... darkness: weapon thrown secretly (the anonymous attack on Keats's poetry)

lorn:	wretched
Echoes:	poetic spirits
mock the corse:	deny the corpse
amorous Deep:	the possessively loving underworld of the dead. According to myth, when Adonis died, Persephone, the queen of the underworld, fell in love with him and was reluctant to let him go
vital:	of life
He died . . . blood:	John Milton is seen by Shelley as the father of a line of true poets (including Keats). He was a passionate Protestant republican who, in his blind old age, saw with the restoration of a Catholic monarchy the destruction of all his political and religious hopes
third:	with Homer and Dante, Milton was the third great epic poet
Not all . . . climb:	in stanza 5 Shelley describes more recent poets who, although not of the stature of Milton, have striven to achieve poetic worth (compare stanzas 4 and 5 with stanzas 43–6)
refulgent prime:	at the moment of their greatest brightness
nursling of thy widowhood:	Urania, the Muse of poetry, widowed by the death of Milton, has had to bring up her latest, promising child (Adonais-Keats) on her own
nipt . . . blew:	perished before the blossom could come
Capital:	Rome
charnel:	a building where the bones of the dead are kept
liquid:	pure
Corruption:	decay
eternal Hunger:	decomposition
flocks:	Shelley represents elements such as Dreams, Splendours and Glooms in the imaginative work of Adonais-Keats as sheep, to suit the pastoral tradition of the elegy
lucid:	shining
anadem:	garland
winged reeds:	arrows
barbed fire:	the pain of love's arrow
guarded wit:	rational mind
dying meteor . . . vapour:	a momentary mark is made by the hot object on a cloud (like a vapour trail left by an aircraft)
clips:	embraces, envelops
Morning . . . kindle day:	the cloudy dawn is personified as a mourning maiden whose loosed hair, wet with tears, prevents her eyes (the sun) from showing clearly

Echo:	a nymph who loved the youth Narcissus; because he loved only himself (see line 141) and ignored her, Echo wasted away until she could only echo the sounds she heard around her. According to stanza 15, she loves Adonais even more than she had loved Narcissus, and she becomes even more inarticulate
kindling:	growing
Hyacinth:	a youth loved by Phoebus Apollo (the sun god) and accidentally killed by him
wan . . . sere:	both Hyacinth and Narcissus were turned into flowers bearing their names when they died. The flowers in mourning for Adonais stand pale and withered
ruth:	compassion
nightingale:	a bird distinguished by its beautiful song and celebrated in Keats's 'Ode to a Nightingale'
nourish . . . morning:	according to legend, the eagle could renew its youth by flying towards the sun. Keats had attempted an epic flight in writing *Hyperion*, a name for the sun-god
Albion:	England
curse of Cain:	Cain in the Bible was punished for the murder of his brother Abel by being made to roam the earth with a special mark on his forehead
his head:	the reviewer of Keats's poems
bier:	stretcher on which to carry a corpse
brake:	thicket
brere:	brier bush
trance:	hibernation
leprous:	decayed as with leprosy
flowers of gentle breath:	anemones (the name in Greek means daughters of the wind)
sword . . . sheath:	surely the sword is more precious than its container and the mind more precious than the body
sightless:	invisible
mean:	insignificant
who lends:	life is a portion of time borrowed from death
slake:	relieve the pain
sister's song:	Echo (see line 128)
ambrosial:	divinely fragrant
she sped:	Urania representing poetry is subject to cruelty and malice but poetry continues and is even benevolent. The journey of Urania recalls details of Bion's elegy on Adonis

heartless: disheartened

chained to time: although she is a goddess she is the Muse to mortal men and cannot escape from time

Dare . . . his den: young Keats's poetry acted as a challenge to the savage (unfed) critics

Wisdom . . . shield: in Greek mythology, the hero Perseus, knowing that if he looked directly at the monster Medusa he would die, fought against her using a reflecting shield

full cycle . . . sphere: reached his full maturity as the moon does

wolves . . . ravens . . . vultures: cowardly creatures who prey on the weak and dead (Keats's critics)

like Apollo: as the heroic Apollo killed the dragon Python, Byron had silenced his critics in his poem *English Bards and Scotch Reviewers* (1809)

The sun . . . awful night: the great poet like the sun creates dependent creatures, both critics and imitators. When he dies the lesser talents can be seen for the first time

mountain shepherd: his fellow poets (in the convention of the pastoral elegy)

magic mantles: garments appropriate to poets

Pilgrim of Eternity: Byron, author of *Childe Harold's Pilgrimage*, and admired by Shelley as a seeker of truth

Ierne: Ireland

sweetest lyrist: Thomas Moore (1779–1852) wrote songs describing the miseries of Ireland and attacking England's policies there

frail Form: a poet figure with Shelleyan characteristics. He is similar to the central figure in Shelley's *Alastor*

Actaeon-like: Actaeon while out hunting came suddenly on Diana, the goddess of chastity, bathing; she turned him into a stag and he was pursued and torn apart by his hounds. The poet looks into a mystery and is tormented by his own sensitivity

pardlike: like a leopard, an animal associated with Dionysus, the god of a religion of ecstasy in ancient Greece

superincumbent hour: the oppressive time of Adonais's death

pied: with more than one colour

light spear: the figure is dressed as a disciple of Dionysus with flowers in his hair and a thyrsus, a symbol of fertility, in his hand

partial: intensely involved

accents . . . land: the language of poetry seems foreign to many readers

mien:	appearance
branded ... Christ's:	in the Bible Cain is given a mark of blood on his forehead by God for killing his brother Abel (see line 151), and Christ's forehead is bloody from the crown of thorns given him as a symbol of contempt. Cain is a murderer, Christ is noble and innocent, but both are outcasts from society as is the poet
In mockery:	imitating (like a statue)
He ... the wise:	Leigh Hunt (1784–1859) was a poet but had greater prominence as a radical journalist. He publicised the work of Keats and Shelley, suffered imprisonment for his views, and supported Keats in his illness
viperous:	poisonous (like a snake). In the poem the killer of Adonais-Keats is represented in several ways
nameless worm:	unknown snake (the anonymous critic)
prelude:	Keats's early poem *Endymion* showed promise which elicited encouragement and anticipation from readers except for the reviewer
Live thou:	Shelley warns that the reviewer is punished by having to live with his own guilt
carrion kites:	birds of prey who feed on dead bodies
burning fountain:	the source of all life. Fire was considered by the Greeks to be the purest of the basic elements and most closely related to the spirit
phantoms:	unreal things. Shelley in this stanza reverses the usual views of life and death
calumny:	slander
sparkless ashes:	dull, routine works with no originality
night's sweet bird:	nightingale
plastic stress:	shaping power
successions:	combinations of raw matter
unwilling dross:	resisting material
splendours ... of time:	beautiful creations, such as poems, made by men are like stars in the sky
mortal lair:	earthly place
earthly doom:	Shelley asserts that achievements of the spirit are not destroyed by human adversity or death
inheritors:	poets like Adonais-Keats who died before their quality was recognised
Unapparent:	invisible realm of the spirit
Chatterton:	the poet Thomas Chatterton (1752–70), to whom Keats dedicated *Endymion*, committed suicide at the age of seventeen

Sidney:	Sir Philip Sidney (1554–86), poet and soldier, died of his wounds in battle at the age of thirty-two after giving his water to another soldier
Lucan:	Marcus Armaeus Lucanus (AD39–65), a Roman poet who wrote against tyranny and censorship. At the age of twenty-six he was forced to commit suicide by the tyrant Nero
Oblivion:	lack of fame personified as a positive force
transmitted effluence:	spreading brightness
kingless sphere:	in ancient times it was believed that each planet and star is guided by its own particular spirit, and that the famous on earth become such spirits. Shelley uses this notion and Adonais-Keats goes to occupy Venus (Vesper) which has been dark ('blind') until now, and to contribute to the traditional harmony of the spheres (line 413)
Fond wretch:	foolish creature
Clasp ... brink:	grasp the idea of the earth swinging in space and imagine the empty edges of the universe; from that vastness, return to the world as we know it, and with this perspective a proper knowledge is possible of life and death
Rome ... sepulchre:	Keats was buried in the Protestant Cemetery in Rome
'tis nought ... away:	it is unimportant that so much of Rome's history is buried under ruins. Minds such as that of Adonais-Keats contribute something of lasting worth, and they do not need support from political and religious oppressors to defy time
green access ... smile:	the open grass of the cemetery where Shelley's three-year old son, William, was buried
moulder:	crumble
hoary brand:	a log covered with ash
keen pyramid:	the sharp-edged tomb of the Roman politician Caius Cestius (first century BC)
Pavilioning:	covering, as with a tent
field ... camp of death:	the more recently dead are buried in the cemetery. The Italian for graveyard is *camposanto*, meaning holy field
charge:	occupant
seal ... mind:	if time has allowed the tears of sorrow to dry. Shelley still laments the loss of his son a year and a half earlier
gall:	bitterness

The One ... to speak: what Shelley, following Plato, calls the 'One' is perfection, purity, the absolute, of which earthly reality is an inadequate, distorted and yet beautiful version. This ultimate reality can be known fully only when one has discarded the distortion of life. The most beautiful natural and created things in life are feeble embodiments of the splendour behind them

what still ... wither: in life, the person or object that is precious, draws one near to be suffocated or pushes one away to die. (Shelley voices a deep despair at the possibility of any human happiness)

That light: in the final two stanzas there are many echoes of the opening of *Paradise*, the third part of *The Divine Comedy* by Dante

Benediction: that blessing which the darkening punishment of being born cannot extinguish

web of being: the complicated, ignorant pattern of life

as each are mirrors: each person or aspect of creation reflects, according to its capacity, the divine for which it strives

now beams: the One, containing 'that light', 'that Beauty', 'that Benediction', 'that sustaining love', appears bright to Shelley, burning away his earthly ignorance

The breath: inspiration (see Shelley's 'Ode to the West Wind', written two years earlier)

bark: small boat with sails

trembling throng: crowd of scared people

massy ... riven: the solid earth and starry sky are torn by the storm

---

'To Edward Williams'

The poem was written on 26 January 1822 and published in 1834. The poet begins by saying that he must separate himself from the very things which can comfort him. Many emotional situations may be tolerated but, without love, the mind becomes ill. To exclude himself too suddenly from his friends would be too drastic, but he finds it increasingly difficult to live a life of deception. His home situation is unclear but also uncomfortable. Other creatures achieve relief and peace but death seems his only hope. Words do not solve the problem but the sympathy of his friends is all he can look for.

COMMENTARY: Shelley wrote the poem as a letter to Edward and Jane Williams (see note below) during a period of coldness between his wife, Mary, and himself. It is an intimate, personal letter and as such Shelley did not intend that it should be made public. Also, as is commonly true of private letters, it has no obvious organised progression. No very clear picture emerges of Edward and Jane Williams and the poem is centred on Shelley's own condition. The single question is addressed to himself and he does not directly ask anything from his friends. Although Shelley's depression and loneliness are emphasised, the poem is saved from being heavily melancholy by the conversational charm he succeeds in introducing.

Throughout the poem, the stanza form with its five lines of ten syllables, two of six and one of eight, is manipulated to provide a sense of variety and surprise; the alternating rhymes in the first six lines help to shape the thoughts passing through the poet's mind and each stanza ends firmly with a rhyming couplet.

NOTES AND GLOSSARY:

Edward Williams: Edward Williams and his common-law wife, Jane, arrived in Pisa early in 1821 and gradually Shelley became strongly attracted to Jane. He enjoyed their company and in April 1822 they moved into a floor of the house where the Shelleys lived. Edward was drowned with Shelley

serpent: Shelley was nicknamed 'the Snake' probably because of his slim shape and quick movements and because *bischelli* (Bysshe Shelley) is the Italian for a small snake. In the Bible, after the Fall of man, Satan in the shape of a serpent is excluded from Eden

haunt a bower: frequent a shaded part of the garden

feigned sighs: pretending regret

mitigated pain: relief from his pain

indifferent: insignificant

poison ... good: what should be seen as damaging (for example, self-pity or envy) is accepted as normal

dear friend: the stress on 'friend' is directed at Jane

minister: offer

withdrawn: if the arrow has gone into the flesh beyond the barb, to pull it out could cause dangerous bleeding

idle: empty

mean: small

carnival: pageant with masks

but: except

lot: fortune

various flowers: that is, by counting their petals

Vision: a dream of happiness

sad oracle: his fortune in the flowers suggests that Mary neither loves nor does not love him

crane: a tall bird notable for long migrations
her: Mary Shelley
resolution: decisiveness, strong character
scorner unrelieved: the critic would receive no satisfaction

'To Jane: The Recollection'

Shelley wrote this poem in February 1822 and it was first published as part of 'The Pine Forest of the Cascine, near Pisa' with a companion poem, 'To Jane: the Invitation', in 1824. Memory is called on to record a beautiful walk with Jane through a pine forest close to the sea. The day is bright and calm and Shelley feels enchanted by the situation and particularly by the presence of Jane. In the pools among the trees, the world above is reflected in miniature; and Shelley finds a rare perfection in these images, a perfection associated with his feelings on love, until a sudden, unwanted puff of wind disturbs the unusually clear image.

COMMENTARY: In this final year of Shelley's life, pleasure itself seemed to becomes precarious and a longer-term contentment seemed out of the question. In the opening lines of the poem there is a note of finality in the repetition of 'last' and the mention of an epitaph. The whole experience described is fragile and transient: a small wind can 'blot one dear image out' and the incident happens while 'we paused' before passing on. An element of the miraculous is indicated in lines 17–20 and later in the notion of a 'magic circle' and the 'Elysian glow' (line 74). Nature and Jane jointly effect this enchantment in which Shelley glimpses a richer and a more satisfying dimension than he experiences in his everyday life. The special awareness, however, is circumscribed by the 'frown' (line 8) and the 'envious wind' (line 81).

The poem is nowadays usually printed in five sections or verse paragraphs of different lengths after an eight-line introduction. The introduction has a different rhyme scheme from the rest of the poem and each line has eight syllables. The bulk of the poem is written in quatrains rhyming *a b a b*, with the even lines two syllables shorter than the odd ones. The regularity of the metre and the tidy precision of the rhymes convey a sense of easy contentment corresponding to the peace felt by the poet.

NOTES AND GLOSSARY:
Jane: Jane Williams (see note on Edward Williams, p. 42)
wonted: customary
epitaph: a brief statement commemorating a dead person
waste: uncultivated area
rude: wild
interlaced: twisted round each other

azure: serene (but also suggesting the bright blue of the clear sky)

As tender . . . own: the pine trees share the calmness and gentle colours of the sky

Ocean woods: growths of seaweed in the depths of the ocean

Made stiller: the sharp tapping of the woodpecker emphasised the quietness

inviolable: impossible to be broken

The breath . . . grew: their very breathing was part of the stillness around them

interfused: intermingled, blended

bound: held or restrained

mortal nature's strife: the turmoil of human life

fair form: Jane Williams

Gulfed: sunk or cut into

firmament: expanse of sky

boundless: infinite, bottomless

There lay: reflected in the pool

lawn: grass

water's love: as if the pool, like a lover, is demonstrating its affection and respect

Elysian: the Elysian Fields in Greek mythology were the dwelling-place of the blessed after death

breast: surface (but continuing the image of human love)

lineament: feature, shape

more than truth exprest: the water magnifies, clarifies, gives extra mystery to, and frames the scene around, so that the scene is enhanced in its reflection

envious: grudging the perfection and peace (very likely Mary Shelley joined the walk and showed her disapproval of Shelley's feelings for Jane)

too faithful: the mind like the water is capable of a heightened awareness. Possibly Shelley felt, also, that he was being irrationally faithful to his wife when she no longer seemed to love him

———'s: Shelley leaves his name out because he is writing a secret love letter

---

'To Jane (The keen stars were twinkling)'

Shelley wrote this poem in June 1822 and it was first published in 1832. He describes Jane playing the guitar at night and how her singing gives life to the notes. She must repeat her song because it opens Shelley's eyes to a superior world.

COMMENTARY: In a letter, Shelley relates how he went sailing with Edward and Jane Williams:

> Williams is captain, and we drive along this delightful bay in the evening wind, under the summer moon, until earth appears another world. Jane brings her guitar, and if the past and future could be obliterated, the present would content me so well that I could say with Faust to the passing moment, 'Remain, thou, thou art so beautiful.'

The intimation at the end of the poem of a world where 'music and moonlight and feeling/Are one' pulls together all the earlier strands, but Shelley insists that such a world of harmony can be called into being only by virtue of the 'dear voice' of the human girl. Without the imaginative feeling provided by the singer, the 'tinkling' notes of the guitar, like the 'twinkling' light of the stars, remain cold and empty.

The verse is deftly controlled with the three different lengths of line and their rhymes being repeated in each stanza. The tripping effect of unstressed syllables in the long lines and the arrested movement in the very short lines suggest the phrasing and shifts of pace and emphasis of guitar music.

NOTES AND GLOSSARY:

keen: sharp (light)

strings without soul: the notes on the guitar have no life of their own (compare the 'cold' light of the stars)

dews: suggests a liquid and pure quality in her voice

overpowers: is emotionally overwhelming

tone: sound, indication

'Lines Written in the Bay of Lerici'

This poem, which is probably unfinished, was written in the second half of June 1822 and first published in 1862. In the opening six lines the moon is addressed. Shelley's attention then shifts to his memory of an evening visit by Jane Williams. For a time after her departure he remains in the pleasing atmosphere she had created, but doubts creep in. He looks at the boats moving out in the bay and, fancifully, imagines that they can cross to another world. The beauty of the day is still there to be felt but the poem concludes with a bitter image of fish being seduced into death.

COMMENTARY: In what must have been one of his very last poems, Shelley manifests a mixture of sweetness and bitter resignation typical of his work in 1822. In the end, he concedes that pleasing sensations are not sufficient, that human pleasure always leaves a sad aftertaste, and that peace or a sense of completion and belonging cannot last for him. The fish is lured to the fisherman by the lamp and is killed; for the human being, however, according to Shelley, there is no clean death when he pursues a dream of love or peace. Shelley presents himself as being ill, and although he dreams of finding relief and describes Jane as a healer and a guardian angel, his opening address to the moon as a 'fair coquette' implies that men are seduced into misery in their very pursuit of constancy. The pain in the poem is balanced by the beautiful images of the moon like a sleeping albatross, the boats like fairy crafts and the tranquil delights of the evening.

Most of the lines have three or four heavy stresses and rhyme in pairs. By varying the pattern of stresses and the units of punctuation, Shelley ensures that the poem advances smoothly but unmechanically. The drama tightens and relaxes and the whole poem has a musing, conversational quality as Shelley's mind moves between his present situation and his memories, what he has and what he misses.

NOTES AND GLOSSARY:

Bay of Lerici: the Bay of Lerici (pronounced 'Léreechee') is on the northwest coast of Italy. Shelley was drowned nearby in the following month

wanderer: moon

coquette: a woman who uses her charm to gain affection but without committing herself, a flirt

To whom . . . for ever: the moon changes its shape and position all the time but is reverenced as a goddess

true: constant

steep: height

albatross: a large, white sea bird capable of flying long distances with its gliding flight; reputed to sleep in the air

chambers: spaces, bedrooms

notes: of music

Haunt: are heard repeated in

o too much: the pleasure is overwhelming

vibration of her touch: Jane practised hypnosis on Shelley by stroking his brow and he felt that her treatment lessened his pains

fancy . . . claim: what he wants from her in his imagination

passions: desires and strivings

alone: entirely

demon: spirit of worry and desire

spirit-winged chariots: vehicles of the gods

serenest element: very calm substance

ministrations: acts of giving aid

Elysian: in Greek mythology, Elysium is the place of complete happiness beyond death

medicine: treat, cure
winged: gave power, pushed
delusive: deceiving
Too happy ... peace: very happy are those persons who, like the fish, seek to satisfy their desires and either die in doing so or destroy the feeling and worry that others have to suffer as part of the pleasure; they pursue a sensation and do not bother with its consequences

Part 3

Commentary

IN AN INTRODUCTORY BOOK on this scale it is not possible to examine Shelley's longer and more complex poems. The selection of poems chosen for consideration does, however, offer examples of the poet's variety, and after studying them the student can move more easily to the more ambitious poems. It is useful to see these poems in an overall view of Shelley's ideas and his development as a poet.

Shelley's ideas and themes

1. Shelley's general attitude

Contrary to his main traditional reputation as a lyric poet, a poet of feelings, Shelley was an intensely intellectual person. From very early in his life, he maintained that every belief, whether it concerned the nature of God or morality, is open to rational discussion and that habit and convention do not in themselves justify a particular form of behaviour. He read widely in the literature and philosophy of all the major languages of Europe, ancient and modern, and the very width of his reading caused him to see how partial the views of one particular time or society could be.

In the Greek writings of the sixth and fifth centuries BC, particularly those of the tragic dramatists and of Plato, Shelley found a fascinating enquiry into human values. Aeschylus (525–456BC) and Sophocles (496–406BC) in their plays present individual man as bound to a fate determined by the gods; in this lack of freedom he cannot seek happiness but must learn to accept what is laid down for him. Paradoxically, in enduring their harsh destinies the characters achieve a grim nobility. Throughout his career, Shelley saw the rational force of this view that the world is as it is, and that individual choice has no effect on the predetermined pattern. In his Notes to the early poem *Queen Mab* (1813), he expounds the doctrine of Necessity and states:

> Every human being is irresistibly impelled to act precisely as he does act: in the eternity which preceded his birth a chain of causes was generated, which, operating under the name of motives, make it impossible that any thought of his mind, or any action of his life, should be otherwise than it is.

Such an inflexible notion, Shelley came to feel was morally abhorrent: it renders all idealism open to a charge of self-deception. The idealism in Plato's writings based on self-knowledge and a pursuit of truth proved powerfully attractive to Shelley. In his poem *Julian and Maddalo* (1818) he explores this very problem of human freedom. Julian, a figure similar to Shelley himself, argues:

> it is our will
> That thus enchains us to permitted ill –
> We might be otherwise – we might be all
> We dream of, happy, high, majestical.
> Where is the love, beauty, and truth we seek
> But in our mind? And if we were not weak
> Should we be less in deed than in desire?

At the end of the poem, however, the problem remains unresolved.

Prometheus Unbound, which derives its opening situation from *Prometheus Bound* by Aeschylus, is a drama on a cosmic scale where the figure of Prometheus, acting as a model for progressive thought, sets himself against the tyrannical power of Jupiter. Liberation from the tyrant comes about as a result of moral pressures in co-operation with the operations of Demogorgon, a shadowy power who seems to represent the cycle of inevitable change or Necessity.

In his Preface to *Prometheus Unbound*, Shelley states that Plato not Aeschylus is his model for human values. Many of Plato's writings have Socrates, his philosophical master, as their central figure and in Shelley's final poem, *The Triumph of Life*, he sees only two persons, Socrates and Jesus, whose lives were strong enough to keep them from being crushed by the chariot of the relentless process of change. It may seem strange that Shelley who was notorious as an atheist should value Jesus so highly, but he made an absolute distinction between the teachings of Jesus which he admired and the practice of organised Christianity which he detested. Jesus and Socrates, according to Shelley, were the victims of repressive and reactionary groups in their societies who could not tolerate the free enquiry initiated by them. Although the Bible remained one of Shelley's favourite books he could not accept any theology implied in it or read into it by others, and he insisted on seeing Jesus as a superior human being and not as a god. He could find no evidence in the world of fact to support a belief in personal survival after death, but in many of his poems, most notably *Adonais*, he appears to argue for a spiritual continuation of wisdom from one generation to the next.

He was well read in science and saw scientific advances as exciting prospects for the betterment of mankind. It never occurred to him that the arts were to be seen as something different from the sciences; the accurate description of a cloud or an understanding of the behaviour of a gas was a part of his knowledge as significant and stimulating as any aesthetic pleasure. He tried to see life as a whole but realised the limitations set by ignorance, habit and fear. In a period of rapid advance in experiment and speculation he saw as a tragedy that 'We have more moral, political and historical wisdom than we know how to reduce into practice; we have more scientific and economic knowledge than can be accommodated to the just distribution of the produce which it multiplies.'

2. Society, politics and change

Shelley was a revolutionary in the sense that he wished for the complete transformation of society in Europe. His antagonism to the existing system began when he was a pupil at Eton:

I do remember well the hour which burst
My spirit's sleep: a fresh May-dawn it was,
When I walked forth upon the glittering grass,
And wept, I knew not why; until there rose
From the near schoolroom, voices, that, alas!
Were but one echo from a world of woes –
The harsh and grating strife of tyrants and of foes.

And he vowed:

                    I will be wise,
And just, and free, and mild, if in me lies
Such power, for I grow weary to behold
The selfish and the strong still tyrannise
Without reproach or check.

These lines appear in the Dedication he wrote to his wife, Mary, for his poem *The Revolt of Islam* in 1817; originally the poem had a sub-title, 'The Revolution of the Golden City: A Vision of the Nineteenth Century', and the poet's political ambition was as large as this title suggests. The French Revolution beginning in 1789 and the ensuing wars in Europe up to 1815 provoked much thought in the idealistic poet. He saw with considerable clarity and great pain that the good elements in the Revolution were defeated and that the old corrupt order had the power to re-establish itself. If this pattern of events was typical, how could good government ever be established? Was force, bloodshed, necessary to defeat evil?

Shelley understood from his knowledge of history, from the Greek city states in the time of Socrates down to the present, that there is no tidy progression from barbarism to humane society. He believed that justice is self-evident and people can be persuaded rationally to see its worth; equally, however, he knew that very few people in positions of power and privilege over other people choose to yield their advantage in the general interest. Those people with scruples are always at a disadvantage to those who have none. In *The Revolt of Islam*, when the good revolutionaries gain power by persuading the populace and the soldiers of their good sense, they decide to forgive their previous oppressors, thus allowing them to re-group; and when the counter-revolution takes place the rulers and priests waste no time in exterminating the revolutionaries. By conviction Shelley was a pacifist, and he saw, with astute penetration, that to adopt evil weapons – even temporarily – is to become the very thing you oppose. A wish for revenge is the ultimate weakness in the revolutionary. In Revolutionary France, the law of the guillotine created the Terror but, asks Shelley, what else could have been expected?:

> Could they listen to the plea of reason who had groaned under the calamities of a social state according to the provisions of which one man riots in luxury whilst another famishes for want of bread? Can he who the day before was a trampled slave suddenly become liberal-minded, forbearing and independent?

In *Prometheus Unbound* the situation of persecution and enmity can only be altered when Prometheus, the victim, withdraws his curse on the despot, Jupiter. Even then he is made to waver by the thought that the very good offered to man is corrupted into the greatest evil. At the end of the poem, with the despot overthrown and after Shelley's visionary description of what the new free condition might be like, the concluding advice acknowledges that the work is still to be done in our ordinary world:

> To suffer woes which Hope thinks infinite;
> To forgive wrongs darker than death or night;
> To defy Power, which seems omnipotent;
> To love, and bear; to hope till Hope creates
> From its own wreck the thing it contemplates;
> Neither to change, nor falter, nor repent

It is clear from many statements in his poetry and prose that Shelley saw revolution not as a sudden solution to the problem but as a long-term process. Central to this process is the education of the people towards a fuller understanding of freedom. Habits of thought, of superiority and inferiority, are so engrained that, Shelley says, it would require the 'systematic efforts of generations of men of intellect and virtue' to change them. He recognised that it is not a substantial advance to abolish the monarchy and the aristocracy if another class is able to step into the same positions of privilege and power. Around him he could see industrialists, landowners, lawyers, merchants and bankers gaining control over people's lives and establishing a 'new aristocracy which has its basis in fraud'. As a committed republican, he urged reform of the voting system as an immediate way by which more people could have more say in the national and international policies of the government. Again, he felt that education was a key to true democracy; until people had some understanding of the issues of politics, a mature and unselfish society could not be created. One of the perennial questions concerning social change is: does reform begin with the structures of society or does reform begin in the minds of individual people? Shelley undoubtedly favoured the second approach, but as he grew older he became increasingly aware that such a gradual programme might, for all its honesty, be futile.

A quarter of a century before the European revolutions of 1848 and the publication of the Communist Manifesto by Karl Marx and Friedrich Engels, Shelley in the last two years of his life described Europe as entering

> the age of the war of the oppressed against the oppressors, and every one of those ringleaders of the privileged gangs of murderers and swindlers, called Sovereigns, look to each other for aid against the common enemy, and suspend their mutual jealousies in the presence of a mightier fear.

Although he welcomed the new self-awareness in the people, he felt apprehensive about the prospect of open class warfare. Hatred and envy would perpetuate the very divisions Shelley wanted to educate society away from. Unlike the later Marxists, he did not give priority to equality or joint ownership of property but saw the crucial issue as equality of rights, rights to live freely, earn a decent living, improve oneself; sharing of wealth would result from the development of a better educated, more just and less materialistic community.

Until fairly recently, many critics, who had read only the commonly anthologised poems by Shelley, dismissed his political views as vague or simplistic or glibly utopian. A more thorough study of his poetry and prose renders such opinions untenable. Shelley involved himself in political affairs as a young man and he offers a shrewd, detailed policy on such matters as an income tax and a system of communal welfare. In his poetry, when he chooses to include it, the observant detail is there:

> a brick house or wall
> Fencing some lonely court, white with the scrawl
> Of our unhappy politics.

and

> Hell is a city much like London –
>   A populous and a smoky city;
> There are all sorts of people undone,
> And there is little or no fun done;
>   Small justice shown, and still less pity . . .
>
> There is a great talk of revolution –
>   And a great chance of despotism –
> German soldiers – camps – confusion –
> Tumults – lotteries – rage – delusion –
>   Gin – suicide – and methodism.

It is true, however, that much of Shelley's political poetry is of a visionary sort, an imagining of how life could be different from the present dissentions and injustices. He felt a duty to nourish the hopes of his contemporaries that a better time could come. He had seen many of his liberal contemporaries become reactionary through their disappointment at the failures of the French Revolution. The stanzas about London quoted above come from his satire on Wordsworth, *Peter Bell the Third*; he satirises the actuality of London so as to strengthen the case for reform. If Shelley was dejected at Wordsworth's loss of political faith, he felt elevated by the example of Milton (see *Adonais*, stanza 4) who, in his blind old age, saw all his political and religious ideals shattered by the Restoration of the monarchy but wrote on defiantly of an eventual victory.

---

3. Love

> Many a green isle needs must be
> In the deep wide sea of Misery,
> Or the mariner, worn and wan,
> Never thus could voyage on –
> Day and night, and night and day,
> Drifting on his dreary way.

In 'Lines Written Among the Euganean Hills', Shelley restates his belief that, politically and personally, there must be places of happiness, times of security and enjoyment. Hope, according to the poet is an essential aspect of human thought which must be carefully cultivated and maintained; behind Hope lies a capability of love which Shelley sees as central to all humane life. What does he mean by Love? In his fragment 'On Love', he writes:

> It is that powerful attraction towards all that we conceive, or fear, or hope beyond ourselves, when we find within our own thoughts the chasm of an insufficient void and seek to awaken in all things that are

a community with what we experience within ourselves. If we reason, we would be understood; if we imagine, we would that the airy children of our brain were born anew within another's; if we feel, we would that another's nerves should vibrate to our own.

Almost certainly this was written about the same time (1815) as he wrote *Alastor*, and in that poem Shelley shows that he sees a weakness in such a view of love. The lonely figure in the poem projects his love of himself or his need for love on to a creature of his fantasy. Throughout his life, Shelley was aware of a confusion between love of himself and a love for someone as that person actually is. In his final poem, *The Triumph of Life*, he presents the figure of the French thinker Rousseau (see Introduction), for whom he had a greater admiration than for any other modern philosopher, as being fatally flawed because, as Rousseau says, 'I was overcome/By my own heart alone'.

In order to avoid this false love, this self-love looking for its own reflection, two things, according to Shelley, are needed: self-knowledge and the ability to enter into the situation of another person. In his 'Defence of Poetry', written in 1821, he writes:

The great secret of morals is love, or a going out of our own nature and an identification of ourselves with the beautiful which exists in thought, action, or person, not our own. A man, to be greatly good, must imagine intensely and comprehensively; he must put himself in the place of another and of many others; the pains and pleasures of his species must become his own.

On the large scale of *Prometheus Unbound*, the poet shows an amazing capability of entering into a comprehensive range of human emotions, the abject and the triumphant, the fearful and the delighted, the malicious and the generous. Asia, the partner of Prometheus, is emblematic of love and her contribution is vital to the process of mankind's regeneration envisaged at the end of the Third Act of the drama.

At the more local level of personal relations, there are many poems. The circumstances of Shelley's two marriages, the unconventional nature of his household and his association with the licentious Lord Byron gave him a considerable notoriety. He certainly added to the speculation by his own pronouncements on the subject of marriage and sexual love. In the poem *Epipsychidion*, which appeared anonymously in 1822, occur the lines:

I never was attached to that great sect,
Whose doctrine is, that each one should select
Out of the crowd a mistress or a friend,
And all the rest, though fair and wise, commend

To cold oblivion, though it is the code
Of modern morals, and the beaten road
Which those poor slaves with weary footsteps tread,
Who travel to their home among the dead
By the broad highway of the world, and so
With one chained friend, perhaps a jealous foe,
The dreariest and the longest journey go.

Despite his own two marriages, Shelley was opposed to marriage as a legal tie and felt that relationships between the sexes should be based on love, mutual respect and mutual care. Certainly in his poetry he gives a particular prominence to women; in many of his political poems a special responsibility rests on a female figure, and women are not patronised or demeaned in his ideas of the good society. In his love poems, however, there is as much regret as celebration, and the poignancy of a disappointed ideal is characteristic of many of his best songs.

Love, both at a personal level and in relation to the advancement of a society, presented Shelley with a challenge to his own narrowness and a means to transcend the loneliness and frailty of individual achievement. Love is the power which Shelley places beyond 'Fate, Time, Occasion, Chance and Change'.

4. Nature

Towards the end of the eighteenth century a change in fashion occurred (see Introduction) and, since that time, educated people have taken pleasure in exploring the world of unspoiled nature. Shelley went to Italy because it was claimed that the climate would help his poor health, and certainly he spent much of his time in the open air. He enjoyed walking and sailing and, although he could not swim, he loved being in the water. According to Mary Shelley, he 'knew every plant by its name, and was familiar with the history and habits of every production of the earth; he could interpret without a fault each appearance in the sky; and the various phenomena of heaven and earth filled him with deep emotion'.

Notwithstanding his knowledge of the natural world, and it coincided with considerable developments in the scientific study of such matters, there are very few poems or even passages of poems in his work concerned with a straightforward description of scenery or plants or animals. What seem to be more interesting to Shelley in his poems are the forces in nature. These forces, whether gentle or destructive, are mysterious to the human mind and Shelley uses our common feeling of bafflement to indicate various limitations in our general understanding. 'Mont Blanc', 'The Ode to the West Wind' and 'The Cloud' are examples of such a use of nature. In 'The Cloud', the transience of clouds and their constant reconstitution from their basic elements of air and water suggest an image of eternal regeneration which we recognise but which, as human beings, we suspect is not true in an ordinary sense for us. At times, however, particularly in unfinished fragments, he offers beautifully observed glimpses of nature without any elaborate extension of its significance. 'Evening: Ponte al Mare, Pisa', 'The Boat on the Serchio' and 'The Aziola', all written in 1821, illustrate this ability:

The sun is set; the swallows are asleep;
The bats are flitting fast in the grey air;
The slow soft toads out of damp corners creep,
And evening's breath, wandering here and there
Over the quivering surface of the stream,
Wakes not one ripple from its summer dream.

Most commonly, happenings in nature provide equivalents for human situations. In 'The Sensitive Plant' (1820) the solitary plant of the title (based on a variety of mimosa which appears to shrink at the approach of humans) is tended with the other flowers in a garden by a beautiful solitary lady. When she dies, all the plants in the garden die but after the winter the weeds return. The poem is enigmatic but seems to suggest that beautiful creatures such as poets are fated to perish by their very sensitivity; the coarse weeds survive. In the Conclusion, however, Shelley wonders if, as the garden is a charade, death is also unreal, and beauty and love do endure although we fail to understand because we are tricked by the charade. In *Alastor* (1815), where a solitary youth travels on and on in pursuit of a figure of his fantasy, the landscapes through which he moves are representative of his obsession and his enclosedness.

At the end of *Alastor*, the poet figure is dead and Shelley sees the death as absolute and offering no consolation. By the time that he wrote *Adonais* (1821), however, he had altered in his philosophy and he came to see a consolation in the cycle of nature. In stanza 42, the physically dead Adonais is 'made one with Nature' and survives as part of a pattern underlying ordinary lives. Shelley, in his own troubled life, obviously found some refreshment in peaceful natural surroundings, and in his mature poetry happiness is always presented in a context of idyllic nature. His vision of human development in *Prometheus Unbound* sees man reconciled with the forces of nature, not struggling against them but moving with them. In his autobiographical poem *Epipsychidion*, written when his marriage with Mary was experiencing a bleak period, he imagines a joyful relationship, away from his current turmoil, on a Greek island 'Within that calm circumference of bliss'. Such wishful thinking apart, Shelley consistently sets his lyrics out of doors and he speculated as to whether the greatness of Greek thought could be attributed to the outdoor lives led by the Greeks.

5. Shelley's view of the poet

In English, a confusion often exists between the words 'verse' and 'poetry'. 'Verse' is a regular, metrical arrangement of words and is recognisably different from prose. 'Poetry' is a more complicated matter and often has an evaluative element. According to Shelley, what distinguishes poetry from other kinds of writing is an imaginative impulse and not a specific form; he refused to accept a distinction between poets and prose writers. It so happens that most of Shelley's favourite poets did write in verse, but not all did. His list would include the Greeks Homer (eighth century BC), Aeschylus, Sophocles, Plato; the Bible, especially the books of Job, Psalms, Isaiah and the New Testament; Dante; Shakespeare; Milton; and of his contemporaries, Wordsworth, Byron and Goethe. He admired high ambition in art and was not interested in social entertainers or witty craftsmen. We can find out about Shelley's thinking on the subject of poetry not only from his poems but from the Prefaces he wrote for most of his longer poems, his letters in which he comments on literature and, most of all, from his 'Defence of Poetry', an essay (unfortunately unfinished) written in 1821.

How, according to him, does a person become a poet? 'A Defence of Poetry' begins with a general description of how the mind works (compare 'Mont Blanc' and 'The Ode to the West Wind'):

> Man is an instrument over which a series of external and internal impressions are driven like the alternations of an ever-changing wind over an Aeolian lyre which move it by their motion to ever-changing melody. But there is a principle within the human being, and perhaps within all sentient beings, which acts otherwise than in a lyre and produces not melody alone but harmony, by an internal adjustment of the sounds and motions thus excited by the impressions which excite them.

Poets are those who seek to prolong and perpetuate these 'adjustments' in words: 'Their language is vitally metaphorical; that is, it marks the before unapprehended relations of things and perpetuates their apprehension until the words which represent them become, through time, signs for portions or classes of thoughts.' Shelley insists that the sounds as well as the sense of the words have to achieve a memorable pattern for the adjustment to be considered a poem.

Shelley's view of the poet may seem abstract, but he was aware that most poetry is stimulated by pleasure or pain and that certain people become poets because of their peculiar sensitivity which sets them apart:

The poet is a nightingale who sits in darkness and sings to cheer its own solitude with sweet sounds; his auditors are men entranced by the melody of an unseen musician, who feel that they are moved and softened, yet know not whence or how.

A similar image appears throughout his poetry from *Alastor*, through 'To a Skylark' where the poet is 'hidden/In the light of thought', to *Adonais*. Not that he advocates that the poet should be a figure remote from ordinary human problems; rather, because of the poet's imaginative insight and gift for language, he sees poetry as the expression and exploration of the deepest aspirations, delights and fears of men and women. In the section on Love (see above), a passage from 'A Defence of Poetry' was quoted, beginning, 'The great secret of morals is love'. Shelley continues:

The great instrument of moral good is the imagination; and poetry administers to the effect by acting upon the cause. Poetry enlarges the circumference of the imagination by replenishing it with thoughts of ever new delight, which have the power of attracting and assimilating to their own nature all other thoughts and which form new intervals and interstices whose void forever craves fresh food.

He conceded that he had 'a passion for reforming the world' but insisted that the appeal of poetry operates through the imagination and not through preaching at the reader; 'didactic poetry is my abhorrence'. Good poetry is not shackled to a set of beliefs, a country or a time, but is available to all. The poet's experience of life should be wide enough to avoid petty emotion and parochial sentiment. Each generation of readers can find new vitality and delight in the work of poets long dead:

Poetry defeats the curse which binds us to be subjected to the accident of surrounding impressions . . . . It makes us the inhabitants of a world to which the familiar world is a chaos . . . . It purges from our inward sight the film of familiarity which obscures from us the wonder of our being.

Because of the centrality he grants to the imagination and because, through their access to imagination, poets manifest a wisdom which forms the basis for all social progress, Shelley feels justified in ending 'A Defence of Poetry' on a militant note:

Poets are the hierophants of an unapprehended inspiration; the mirrors of the gigantic shadows which futurity casts upon the present; the words which express what they understand not; the trumpets which sing to battle and feel not what they inspire; the influence which is moved not, but moves. Poets are the unacknowledged legislators of the world.

Shelley's style

1. Verse

From his reading of ancient and modern literatures, Shelley developed a comprehensive knowledge of the forms verse had taken. In the history of English poetry, few poets can rival him in the variety of verse forms exemplified in his work. It is typical of this variety that, of the poems considered in Part 2, no two have the same verse form. 'Ozymandias' and 'England in 1819' are both sonnets but they have different rhyme schemes and internal divisions. It could be said that 'The Mask of Anarchy' and 'Lines Written in the Bay of Lerici' both use rhyming couplets; the differences, however, are much more striking than a superficial similarity. What is meant by the term 'verse form'? It includes the length of lines, the distribution of stressed and unstressed syllables (metre), the repetition of rhyme sounds (rhyme scheme), the groupings of lines by spacing or even punctuation: in short, verse form is the distribution of the words of a poem into a visual and auditory pattern. In 'A Defence of Poetry', Shelley discusses this subject:

> Sounds as well as thought have relation both between each other and towards that which they represent, and a perception of the order of these relations has always been found connected with a perception of the order of those relations of thoughts. Hence the language of poets has ever affected a certain uniform and harmonious recurrence of sound, without which it were not poetry, and which is scarcely less indispensable to the communication of its influence than the words themselves, without reference to that peculiar order.

Why does the poet choose a particular verse form for a poem? First of all, the 'poem' does not exist in the poet's mind in some amorphous condition waiting to be poured into the mould of a verse form. As Shelley tries to explain in the quotation above, the form and the content need each other and have life only with each other. It is certainly true that some verse forms have proved very fitting for certain subjects or certain treatments of subjects; on the other hand, some forms have been used so brilliantly or so often that a poet becomes reluctant to dare to use them. In his Preface to *The Revolt of Islam*, Shelley discusses his choice of the stanza which he later used again in *Adonais*:

> I have adopted the stanza of Spenser (a measure inexpressibly beautiful), not because I consider it a finer model of poetical harmony than the blank verse of Shakespeare and Milton, but because in the latter there is no shelter for mediocrity; you must either succeed or fail. This perhaps an aspiring spirit should desire. But I was enticed

also by the brilliancy and magnificence of sound which a mind that
has been nourished upon musical thoughts can produce by a just and
harmonious arrangement of the pauses of this measure.

His mention of music is revealing and it becomes obvious to anyone who
studies the manuscript drafts of Shelley's poems that some of them
began as much as sounds or tunes in his head as they did as ideas. In fact,
sometimes the tune seems complete in his head but there remain blank
spaces in the words.

In Part 2 a justification is offered for the verse form used in the poems
under discussion. The form adopted has to be appropriate to the subject
matter, the tone of voice of the speaker and the pace of reading expected
from a reader and, particularly in a long poem, it has to be adaptable
enough to be flexible to the shifts in the poem. *The Revolt of Islam* is a
long poem (almost five thousand lines) but the Spenserian stanza is
supple enough to carry without strain what is basically a narrative
content. In *Prometheus Unbound*, however, described by Shelley as a
'lyrical drama', rhyming verse of many different forms is used to provide
variety in speed and characterisation from the rather monumental blank
verse spoken by the main characters. Choral effects of one 'voice' of
verse played off against another give a sense of a stereophonic drama
gradually moving from conflict to the harmony of a universal
agreement. Such elaborate techniques are not reserved for the large-
scale poems; a re-reading of 'The Ode to the West Wind' or 'To Jane
(The keen stars were twinkling)' will prove the same subtle interaction of
form and content. 'The Cloud' is a splendid example of versifying
virtuosity where longer and shorter lines, end of line rhyme and internal
rhyme, alliterations and assonances, a flurry of unstressed syllables
between even stresses, all help to communicate the mischievous,
inventive, many-mooded, always changing but triumphantly permanent
character of the cloud.

2. Language

Just as the poet has to choose a verse form appropriate to his material,
so he has to exploit the resources of language in the interests of clarity of
communication, vividness, variety and pleasure. Among these resources
are the range of his vocabulary (sometimes called diction), the
arrangement of words in sentences (syntax) with the help of
punctuation, and a particular form of vocabulary, imagery, which will
be considered in the following section.

As regards diction, Shelley states his position in the Preface to his play
The Cenci (1819):

I entirely agree with those modern critics [he is thinking specifically of
Wordsworth's comments in the Preface to the *Lyrical Ballads*, 1800]

who assert that in order to move men to true sympathy we must use the familiar language of men, and that our great ancestors the ancient English poets are the writers, a study of whom might incite us to do that for our own age which they have done for theirs. But it must be the real language of men in general and not that of any particular class to whose society the writer happens to belong.

What 'the familiar language of men' means is, of course, open to dispute and Shelley's comment, in part, acknowledges the difficulty. It is true of his poetry, however, that, whatever aim he set for his language, the width of his vocabulary and the complexities of his expression are hardly familiar to most readers.

One of the characteristics of his style is his heavy use of abstract words. Some titles are indicative of this tendency: 'Mutability', 'Hymn to Intellectual Beauty', 'Love, Hope, Desire, and Fear', 'Ode to Heaven'. Many readers feel daunted by a line such as, 'O world! O life! O time!' or a passage such as:

> even then
> Two mighty spirits, mingling, made a third
> Mightier than either, which, unbodied now,
> Between us floats, felt, although unbeheld,
> Waiting the incarnation, which ascends.

The abstract words are related to an etherial quality common in his poetry. These lines from *Prometheus Unbound* can be matched with the opening of the 'Hymn to Intellectual Beauty':

> The awful shadow of some unseen Power
> Floats though unseen amongst us, – visiting
> This various world with as inconstant wing
> As summer winds that creep from flower to flower.

How can something unseen cast a shadow? And how can a shadow be unseen? Shelley does not immediately clarify the situation by his introduction of a simile of something else, the 'summer winds', which is just as intangible as the shadow and the Power. Often it might be said of his poetry, as he says of the Witch in *The Witch of Atlas* (1820),

> her beauty made
> The bright world dim, and everything beside
> Seemed like the fleeting image of a shade.

Certainly Shelley was well aware of his inclination to the abstract and the etherial. Mary Shelley writes of him that he had 'no care for any of his poems that did not . . . develop some high or abstruse truth'. His view, often described as Platonic, that the world apprehended through our senses is incomplete, a poor, distorted reflection of a richer world that could be available to our experience, is expressed in his choice of language. Although he was not religious in any orthodox sense, he does use religious language in his attempt to convey his vision of a spiritual dimension beyond the actual; words such as 'Evil', 'Faith', 'Heaven', 'divine', 'Eternity' have the power of their religious associations but are used to support Shelley's secular vision. In 'Hymn to Intellectual Beauty' and elsewhere, he describes how he has come to have this vision where he has glimpsed

> Clear, elemental shapes, whose smallest change
> A subtler language within language wrought.

His problem, to share this 'subtler language', is a central problem for all poets: he uses the words that are in the dictionary but he must find a way of using them so that the words bear his vision and strike the reader as if they were newly created.

A further difficulty experienced particularly by modern readers concerns Shelley's use of proper names. It is easy to be disconcerted by titles which seem alien to modern life; *Epipsychidion*, *Prometheus Unbound* and *Adonais* all require a translation before a reading can begin. Within twelve lines of the final Chorus of *Hellas* Shelley manages to include 'Hellas', 'Peneus', 'Tempes', 'Cyclads', 'Argo', 'Orpheus', 'Ulysses' and 'Calypso'. For the poet, the people and places of classical Greece were so familiar as to have become aspects of his own mind, as alive and exciting as incidents happening around him. As John Milton does in *Paradise Lost* (1667) and T. S. Eliot in *The Waste Land* (1922), Shelley tries to take a panoramic view of history in which the salient features, the significant achievements, have a timeless and, therefore, contemporary value. In this scheme, he blends his own thinking with mythological patterns derived from his reading, and the result poses problems for readers who do not enjoy this global knowledge; for such readers there is a choice of trying to read what Shelley read or of using reference books. The latter solution is again necessary to help with topical references in Shelley, whether they be to political events, fellow poets, biographical details, or current scientific theories. His traditional reputation as a simple, rather confused lyric poet has done a disservice to him and to his readers. Shelley writes out of the whole of his experience and makes huge intellectual demands on his readers; it is better for readers to begin with this understanding.

On the other hand, he has been attacked by some critics as being other-wordly and as having no grasp of the world of facts and ordinary life; again, this is a very partial view. A glance at some of the poems analysed in Part 2 will show sections of flat description and plain language. The two sonnets are, for the most part, utterly straightforward. A couple of examples from elsewhere in Shelley should help to establish that he can write factually and in everyday language when he chooses. His poem *Julian and Maddalo* begins with these lines:

> I rode one evening with Count Maddalo
> Upon the bank of land which breaks the flow
> Of Adria towards Venice; a bare strand
> Of hillocks, heaped with ever-shifting sand,
> Matted with thistles and amphibious weeds,
> Such as from earth's embrace the salt ooze breeds,
> Is this; an uninhabited sea-side,
> Which the lone fisher, when his nets are dried,
> Abandons.

This description is prosaic and serves to set the scene for a dialogue between the two men of the title. In his 'Letter to Maria Gisborne', written to her in London while he was living in her house in Italy, Shelley writes personally, wittily and observantly about things they have in common. She will recognise the objects he is describing as belonging to her son, Henry, who is an engineer:

> Near that a dusty paint-box, some odd hooks,
> A half-burnt match, an ivory block, three books,
> Where conic sections, spherics, logarithms,
> To great Laplace, from Saunderson and Sims,
> Lie heaped in their harmonious disarray
> Of figures, – disentangle them who may.
> Baron de Tott's Memoirs beside them lie,
> And some odd volumes of old chemistry.

There are many passages in his poems where he writes in a similar conversational style or with a factuality proper to a detailed description.

What are the characteristics of Shelley's syntax, of the ordering of his sentences? Some comments were offered earlier on his punctuation (see 'A note on the text') but certain features are significant parts of his style. He is fond of long sentences, commonly using his stanza as the length of his sentences even when the stanza form he is using may be eight or ten lines long. Colons, semi-colons, dashes and commas hold together what, nowadays, would tend to be divided into several shorter sentences. Obviously, Shelley's thoughts run in larger units than those of most readers and in his mind there is a constant process of qualification, addition, connection and redefinition. Question marks and exclamations are common and convey his curiosity, excitement, doubts and abrupt shifts in thought and feeling. Sometimes, for example in the first sentence in 'Mont Blanc', the impetuous rush of the poet's mind has to be disentangled by the reader and the thoughts re-ordered in a slower sequence. In his dramas Shelley makes an effort, often successful, to shape the syntax as well as the diction in order to make it dramatically appropriate to the character who is speaking in a particular situation.

3. Imagery

A poet's general ideas are made more immediately graspable and vivid by being presented in terms related to the five senses, and it is this mode of presentation that is meant by 'imagery'. Shelley, concerned as he was with such complex intellectual schemes, has a special poetic problem to find an imagery adequate to his vision. In *Prometheus Unbound* the figure of Demogorgon, when asked to identify the source of evil in the universe, declines to offer an answer, saying, 'The deep truth is imageless.' The poet, however, has to try, and several kinds of imagery are characteristic of Shelley's poetry.

The word 'synaesthesia' is used when a quality associated with one sense, say sight, is employed to describe another sense, say sound; for example, a colour may be described as 'loud' or 'hot'. In Shelley, we find dew described as 'melodious', sighs as 'odorous' and warmth as 'sweet' and, in *The Revolt of Islam*, the spiritual and sexual union of Laon and Cythna is related:

> The beating of our veins one interval
> Made still; and then I felt the blood that burned
>> Within her frame, mingle with mine, and fall
>> Around my heart like fire; and over all
> A mist was spread, the sickness of a deep
>> And speechless swoon of joy, as might befall
> Two disunited spirits when they leap
> In union from this earth's obscure and fading sleep.

'Burned', 'mist' and 'speechless' are experienced through different senses but, in a sensibility where 'sweet streams of sunny thoughts and flowers . . . weave their sounds and odours into one', there is no conflict. Related to this blending of the senses, is Shelley's practice of abruptly varying the kind of image he is using to describe a scene or a person; good examples can be found in the opening lines of *The Triumph of Life* and the first stanza of 'Ode to Liberty'. A more obviously organised form of the same technique is where he groups together a series of similes, all likenesses to the same focus of thought. In 'To a Skylark' stanzas 8–11 consist of similes, resemblances to the skylark (see the Commentary on the poem), and a similar cluster of similes is to be found describing the visitation of intellectual beauty in 'Hymn to Intellectual Beauty':

> Like moonbeams that behind some piny mountain shower,
>> It visits with inconstant glance

Each human heart and countenance;
Like hues and harmonies of evening, –
Like clouds in starlight widely spread, –
Like memory of music fled, –
Like aught that for its grace may be
Dear, and yet dearer for its mystery.

The techniques described in this paragraph concede that a deep truth has no neat image by which it can be communicated; instead, the poet offers a series of recognisable experiences which share certain elements, and in these shared elements, in the overlap of the experiences, is some approximation to the abstruse vision enjoyed by the poet. The use of multiple images has been attacked as a confusion, vagueness, diffuseness, but Shelley's method allows profundity to remain something mysterious, untidy, towards which readers have to struggle and towards which there may be different approach roads.

When he distinguishes between good and evil in life, Shelley, again, has no single recognisable image which he can use as a convenient label. He does, however, show certain tendencies. Good qualities are often described in terms of music, bright colours, light, air, sky, water, wind, fire and natural growth, particularly flowers. Most of these elements are included in 'To a Skylark' and the same pattern can be seen whether he is describing love, virtue or liberty. The saving figure in 'The Mask of Anarchy', for example, contains 'light', 'brighter', 'wings', 'sunny rain', 'shower of crimson dew', 'wind', 'air', 'flowers', 'waves'; and in the climactic stanza 52 of *Adonais* the 'One' is described in similar terms. Conversely, evil is associated with animals of prey, graves, worms, decay, blood, darkness, disease and money. In *The Revolt of Islam* and 'The Mask of Anarchy' the evil-doers are presented with these symptomatic emblems, and in these two poems the struggle between good and evil is dramatically enacted through a conflict in the imagery. Shelley does tend to repeat these emblems from poem to poem and it is easy to tire of 'priests who feed on gold and blood' and bright shapes in air-borne vehicles.

In a letter of 1817, he writes that his special interest as a poet is

to apprehend minute and remote distinctions of feeling, whether relative to external nature or to the living beings which surround us, and to communicate the conceptions which result from considering either the moral or the material universe as a whole.

These 'conceptions' lead to Shelley's use of abstract words and these were discussed in the previous section. One way in which he seeks to communicate his conceptions is to personify them – that is, dress them up as dramatic characters. Liberty, Love, Panic, Laws, Earth, Danger, Hope and many other entities are presented as acting out a part in 'the moral or the material universe as a whole'; thus, 'kingly Death keeps his pale court' and Dreams are 'the passion-winged ministers of thought' in *Adonais*. *Prometheus Unbound* is a drama on the largest scale imaginable but it can also be interpreted as being concerned with aspects of the individual mind. To be able to adjust the interpretation in such different ways requires a learned flexibility on the part of the reader. In his Preface to the drama, Shelley acknowledges the difficulty and writes:

> The imagery which I have employed will be found, in many instances, to have been drawn from the operations of the human mind, or from those external actions by which they are expressed. This is unusual in modern poetry, although Dante and Shakespeare are full of instances of the same kind.

Imagery, in this case, comes very close to symbolism and many readers have noticed how, throughout his work, certain major images or symbols recur. Caves, rivers, islands, moonlight, starlight, journeys, the wise old man – all these are associated with the acquisition of wisdom, but Shelley seldom pauses to explain what they represent. Some of them are traditional symbols in the literature of quests but they are not immediately recognisable to every reader. Certain areas from which many poets derive images shared with their readers are not particularly used by Shelley. There are very few images derived from childhood, for example, or from professions and trades or from city life.

Part 4

Hints for study

How to improve your understanding of the poems

(a) Read the poems aloud many times over a period of days or weeks. Pay careful attention to the different combinations of line length, punctuation, rhythm, rhyme and intonation used by the poet and usually what you read with such care will make reasonable sense. Rhyme sounds, stressed syllables and line endings have to be indicated in your reading but they should not sound mechanical or trite.

(b) When you have difficulty in understanding a poem, you can try one of three approaches. First, establish as much as you can concerning the formal arrangement of lines, rhymes, repeated phrases, stanzas, syntax; often the particular arrangement indicates the nature of the poem – whether it is an argument, a satire or whatever. Second, be clear as to the situation behind the poem; for example, a man addressing a woman, a response to a public event, an appeal to an audience, an overheard conversation, an allegorical incident. Third, trace the main elements of imagery employed; the pressure of imagery usually points to and expresses the central concern of the poem.

(c) Use dictionaries and reference books. Clear up any local obscurities caused by unusual words or proper names which are unfamiliar to you.

(d) Write brief summaries of the poems. Few poems are narratives, but to make yourself write such summaries is to force you to attend to the general order of the poem and impress it on your mind.

(e) When you enjoy a line or a passage, make a point of learning it by heart. Such pieces maintain the actuality of the poem in your mind, help you to guard against seeing the poem solely in terms of ideas and provide you with essential evidence for use in examination or essay answers.

(f) Choose passages of about ten lines and mark in the stressed syllables. Check how consistent Shelley is from line to line, whether he varies the stress pattern and why.

(g) Similarly, determine the rhyme scheme in passages of about ten lines and try to work out why Shelley has chosen a particular rhyme scheme and what it contributes to the effect of the passage.

(h) Some attempt should be made to acquaint yourself with the influences on Shelley's thinking and the figures whom he admired. The names of such people mentioned in these Notes should be followed up.

A list of works praised by Shelley would include: Aeschylus, *Prometheus Bound*; Sophocles, *Oedipus the King*; Plato, *The Symposium*; the Bible, Job, some of the Psalms, St John; Dante, *Hell*, Canto 1, and *Paradise*, Canto 1; Shakespeare, *The Tempest*; Milton, *Paradise Lost*, Books 1 and 2; Wordsworth, 'Lines Composed a Few Miles Above Tintern Abbey' and 'Ode: Intimations of Immortality'; Goethe, *Faust*, Part 1; Byron, *Cain*.

(i) Other works by Shelley should be read. Of his poems, *Julian and Maddalo*, *Prometheus Unbound* and *The Triumph of Life* extend your knowledge enormously. You should read from his prose 'A Defence of Poetry', 'An Address to the People on the Death of the Princess Charlotte', 'Essay on Love' and the Preface to *Prometheus Unbound*.

Quotations appropriate to some topics

In Part 3, to illustrate Shelley's ideas, quotations were drawn from all of his work. Some examples are given here, with line numbers, from the poems considered in Part 2; you should add further examples of your own, choosing ones appropriate to each topic.

(1) *Shelley's general attitude*

'Mont Blanc', 1–11 (how the mind works); 'Ozymandias', 12–14 (comment on time and the desert of human vanity); 'To a Skylark', 86–90 (tragic view); *Adonais*, 460–68 (the absolute beyond our lives); 'To Jane (The keen stars were twinkling)', 20–4 (a notion of perfection); 'Lines Written in the Bay of Lerici', 51–8 (image of the deception of pleasure in life).

(2) *Society, politics and change*

'Ozymandias', 10–14 (rebuke to aspirations to power); *The Mask of Anarchy*, 6–49 (description of contemporary power in England); 156–211 (the condition of slavery); 212–65 (the condition of freedom); 372–6 (rallying call to the people); 'England in 1819', 1–12 (description of England under George III); 13–14 (Shelley's hope for change); Ode to the West Wind', 63–70 (appeal to the wind to help bring about a revolution); *Adonais*, 29–36 (the revolutionary Milton).

(3) *Love*
'To a Skylark', 76–80 (sadness of human love); *Adonais*, 163–71 (love and the procreation of nature); 469–77 (bleak view of love on earth); 'To Jane: The Recollection', 41–51 (magic spell of love); 'Lines Written in the Bay of Lerici', 28–32 (suspension of time in love); 51–8 (hopelessness of human love).

(4) *Nature*
'Mont Blanc', 76–83 (power of nature can force man to reconsider his values); 'Ode to the West Wind', 15–23 (destructive power of the wind); 29–36 (beauty of clear water); 'To a Skylark', 56–60 (clean beauty); *Adonais*, 379–87 (creative impulse in nature); 'To Jane: The Recollection', 25–32 (tranquillity of nature); 69–80 (a perfection glimpsed through nature); 'Lines Written in the Bay of Lerici', 7–14 (the moon).

(5) *Shelley's view of the poet*
'Mont Blanc', 41–8 (mystery of poetic inspiration); 139–44 (necessity of the imagination); 'Ode to the West Wind', 57–69 (revolutionary function of the inspired poet); 'To a Skylark', 36–40 (poet writes out of his solitude); 101–5 (prophetic role of the poet); *Adonais*, 274–9 (fated figure of the poet); 379–87 (poet as a creator); 406–14 (eternal realm of art).

Answering questions on poetry

(1) Examine the particular question carefully. Make sure that you understand the wording of the question and what kind of answer it requires. Many questions assume certain values; you may feel that you have to challenge these implied values.

(2) Plan your answer, paragraph by paragraph. Devote your first paragraph to discussing the question and providing any necessary background material. Determine what are to be the main points in your answer, remembering that evidence from the poetry is needed to support your argument. You are trying to persuade the examiner that your view of the poem (and of the question) is justified. Your essay should end with a brief conclusion showing what you have proved.

(3) Quotations are needed to demonstrate that what you assert about the poetry is true. Quotations also give the actual flavour of the poetry in a manner which you cannot describe.

(4) The nature of the poetry should be made evident in your discussion. If the poem is comic or lyrical or dramatic, such a quality must be conveyed in your answer. The overall shape and texture of the poem should be implied in your answer.

(5) Avoid abstract words unless they are absolutely necessary. Write clearly and directly.

(6) Do not repeat the ideas, interpretations or special vocabulary of critics until you are fully persuaded of their validity and have assimilated them.

(7) Remember that the poem is separated from its author by being published; his opinions on it may be interesting or helpful but, eventually, the poem is as it is published. It must explain itself; it . belongs to the readers. Certainly know about the author's life, his period and his other works, but do not add biographical or background material unless it is strictly relevant to the literary question.

A sample answer

It has been claimed that nature is used merely to provide a pretty background to the elegy for Adonais. Discuss this view.

It is difficult to ascertain in what sense the word 'nature' is being used in the question. Does it mean the mention of birds and flowers? Or does it suggest a power, a natural force? In the poem, the word 'nature' occurs twice, once in stanza 31 and once in stanza 42, both times with a capital letter. Different aspects of the natural world, images derived from nature, do, however, appear throughout the poem. It is necessary, first of all, to understand the kind of poem *Adonais* is and then it should be possible to decide what functions nature serves in this scheme.

The poem was written as an elegy on the death of John Keats, but Shelley chose to model his work on examples of the pastoral elegy he knew from Greek literature and John Milton's *Lycidas*. According to the conventions of the pastoral elegy, the dead person is presented as a shepherd whose death is lamented by a fellow shepherd; the setting, therefore, for such an elegy is a natural one and the natural world shares the sense of loss of one of its workers. Shelley abides by the conventions to the extent that Adonais is given 'flocks' ((l. 75), his death is lamented by aspects of the pastoral world (stanzas 14–19) and his fellow poets appear as 'mountain shepherds' (l. 262). These elements of nature are no mere background but constitute a major part of the organising principle of the poem.

Shelley makes his elegy for Keats indirect in another way. At no point is the lamented person referred to as Keats but always as Adonais. The name is derived and developed from Adonis, a beautiful youth who, according to Greek mythology, was loved by the goddess Venus, and when he was killed by a wild boar, lived partly in the underworld of death and partly on earth. In Greek mythology he is associated with the annual death of nature in winter and its resurrection in the spring. Shelley does not tie himself too closely to the mythological story but he uses Adonis's restoration in a transformed shape in the poem. The manner of Adonis's death is also translated by Shelley into the cruel murder of the poet by savage critics. Again he has incorporated into his poem a process of nature in a mythological form.

The pastoral elegy, as Shelley knew from his reading, is not narrowly concerned with lamentation and certainly not with lamentation for the death of one person; rather, it is an opportunity for the poet to show how death can be accommodated in a larger scheme of continuity and value. Equally, the story of Adonis survives because it enacts a pattern of death with renewal. In both the pastoral elegy and the story of Adonis, nature is not simply a location but is the prime example of how what is valued dies but is always renewed with the turning of the year. The most poignant passage in the first half of the poem occurs between stanzas 18 and 21 where, after the death of winter, everything revives except Adonais:

> Ah, woe is me! Winter is come and gone
> But grief returns with the revolving year
>
> (ll. 154–5)

Earlier, aspects of nature had lamented in sympathy for the poet who had in his work celebrated them, but now it appears that the thinking creature, man, alone is doomed to extinction:

> the intense atom glows
> A moment, then is quenched in a most cold response
>
> (ll. 179–80)

Shelley believed that Keats's death had been hastened by aggressive criticism of his poetry and, although he uses various terms with which to attack such critics, most of his terms come from predatory creatures in nature. Among the names of abuse he employs are: 'unpastured dragon' (l. 238); 'monsters of life's waste' (l. 243); 'herded wolves' (l. 244); 'obscene ravens' (l. 245); 'vultures' (l. 246); 'viperous murderer' (l. 317); 'carrion kites' (l. 335). Such creatures suggest to the reader an attack on the healthy, the natural; certainly they do not contribute, as the essay question might imply, to a 'pretty background'.

Of Keats's or Adonais's fellow poets who come as 'mountain shepherds', particular prominence is given to the one who seems to be punished for having presumptuously probed too deeply into nature (stanza 31). This mourner, however, bears the emblems of nature – flowers, a cypress cone and ivy. Shelley may be suggesting that during life human beings cannot merge with the rest of nature and should not try. Whatever the meaning of these difficult stanzas, nature is quite definitely central to man's existence.

In the second half of the poem, from stanza 38, there is a decisive change from the poet, possibly Shelley himself, who feels guilty at having 'gazed on Nature's naked loveliness' (l. 275) to the dead poet who has 'awakened from the dream of life' (l. 344) and who 'is made one with Nature' (l. 370). The poem argues that our views of life and death are very limited and the turning point is reached when Shelley realises that, in death, Adonais can unite with all the best things he aimed at in life. In life the poet feels solitude and separateness; in death he becomes 'a portion of the loveliness/Which once he made more lovely' (ll. 379–80). The Nature of this second half is the manifestation of what underlies our existence. There is one further twist in the poem beyond the union of Adonais with Nature. In stanza 52 Shelley writes:

> The One remains, the many change and pass;
> Heaven's light forever shines, Earth's shadows fly;
> Life, like a dome of many-coloured glass,
> Stains the white radiance of Eternity,
> Until Death tramples it to fragments.

> (ll. 460–4)

The nature that we know on earth is part of the 'dome of many-coloured glass'; we cannot see clearly through it to the ultimate One. Only when we have a perspective bigger than our lives can we glimpse this absolute; the poem concludes paradoxically asserting that only in death can we apprehend reality.

Throughout the poem, there are many beautiful images of nature. Adonais described as a 'broken lily' (l. 54); the procession of Adonais's poetic thoughts 'Like pageantry of mist on an autumnal stream' (l. 117): nature's voices 'from the moan/Of thunder, to the song of night's sweet bird' (ll. 371–2); these examples and many others delight the reader and enhance the charm of the poem. When we consider, however, the aspects of the poem examined in this essay, and the emphasis on the essential part nature plays in man's existence, it seems inadequate to see nature in the poem as merely a 'pretty background to the elegy'.

Questions on the poems in Part 2

(1) Write an account of the 'Ode to the West Wind' showing clearly how Shelley organises and expresses his thoughts.

(2) Describe the imagery of 'To a Skylark' and explain how Shelley uses it in the poem.

(3) What is Shelley enquiring into in 'Mont Blanc'? Does he reach a satisfactory conclusion?

(4) Describe the way in which Shelley presents a political struggle in *The Mask of Anarchy*. Does the outcome seem convincing to you?

(5) 'Ozymandias' and 'England in 1819' are both sonnets. Compare the differences Shelley introduces in the basic form of fourteen lines.

(6) In Shelley's lyrics prompted by Jane Williams, what idea of love emerges?

(7) How does Shelley move from a sense of loss to celebration in *Adonais*?

(8) Choose five stanzas from *Adonais*, show how Shelley varies his handling of the Spenserian stanza, and offer an opinion on how successful he is in each.

(9) How would you defend 'To Edward Williams' against the accusation of self-pity on Shelley's part?

(10) Using the poems examined in Part 2, attempt to describe the main characteristics of Shelley's style.

(11) Describe Shelley's view of the poet as it emerges in 'Ode to the West Wind' and 'To a Skylark'.

(12) Discuss how the ending of 'Lines Written in the Bay of Lerici' fits with the rest of the poem.

(13) 'Mont Blanc' is written in verse paragraphs. Show how Shelley develops his thinking from one part to the next throughout the poem.

(14) 'Mont Blanc' was written in 1816 and 'Lines Written in the Bay of Lerici' was written in 1822. In what ways does Shelley's language seem to have changed (given the very different subjects of the poems)?

(15) What contribution is made to the effect of *The Mask of Anarchy* by the metre and rhyme scheme?

(16) Analyse the ingredients of Shelley's delight and regret in 'To Jane: The Recollection'.

(17) Use the evidence offered by the poems in Part 2 to argue whether or not Shelley has an optimistic outlook on life.

(18) Discuss the different ways in which Shelley employs imagery derived from nature in his poems.

(19) Shelley agreed that he had 'a passion for reforming the world'. What, according to his poems, is wrong with the world and how can it be changed?

(20) Demonstrate how the terza rima verse form is used in 'Ode to the West Wind'. How successful is the poem?

Part 5

Suggestions for further reading

Texts of the poems

The Complete Poetical Works of Percy Bysshe Shelley, edited by Thomas Hutchinson (1904), revised by G. M. Matthews, Oxford University Press, London, 1970.

Shelley: Selected Poems, edited by Timothy Webb, Dent, London, 1977. Clear introduction and sensible notes.

Shelley's Poetry and Prose, selected and edited by Donald H. Reiman and Sharon B. Powers, Norton, New York, 1977. Includes *A Defence of Poetry* and has helpful notes and a number of essays by leading critics.

Shelley's prose

Shelley's Prose: The Trumpet of a Prophecy, edited by David Lee Clark, University of New Mexico Press, Albuquerque, N. Mex., 1966.

The Letters of Percy Bysshe Shelley, edited by F. L. Jones, 2 vols., Clarendon Press, Oxford, 1964.

Biography

HOLMES, RICHARD: *Shelley: The Pursuit*, Weidenfeld & Nicolson, London, 1974. Readable and informative.

TRELAWNY, EDWARD JOHN: *Records of Shelley, Byron, and the Author* (1878), edited by David Wright, Penguin Books, Harmondsworth, 1973. Entertaining if not always reliable account of Shelley, based on personal acquaintance.

Critical books on Shelley

CAMERON, KENNETH NEILL: *Shelley: The Golden Years*, Harvard University Press, Cambridge, Mass., 1974. A good account of Shelley's ideas and preoccupations in relation to his poetry.

CHERNAIK, JUDITH: *The Lyrics of Shelley*, The Press of Case Western Reserve University, Cleveland, Ohio, 1972. Careful texts and a very solid study of the shorter poems.

REIMAN, DONALD H.: *Percy Bysshe Shelley*, Twayne, New York, 1969. A concise account of Shelley's work.

RIDENOUR, GEORGE M. (ED.): *Shelley: A Collection of Critical Essays*, Prentice-Hall, Englewood Cliffs, N.J., 1965. Modern essays, some on topics, some on specific poems.

SWINDEN, PATRICK, (ED.): *Shelley: Shorter Poems and Lyrics*, Macmillan, London, 1976. Essays from the nineteenth and twentieth centuries trace Shelley's reputation and explore difficulties in the shorter poems.

WASSERMAN, EARL: *Shelley: A Critical Reading*, Johns Hopkins University Press, Baltimore, Md., 1971. Very difficult but thorough and rewarding.

WEBB, TIMOTHY: *Shelley: A Voice Not Understood*, Manchester University Press, Manchester, 1977. A clearly written assessment of the poetry showing a sound knowledge of Shelley's reading.

WOODINGS, R. B. (ED.): *Shelley: Modern Judgements*, Macmillan, London, 1968. A selection of essays different from those chosen by Ridenour (see above).

The author of these notes

ALASDAIR D. F. MACRAE was educated at the University of Edinburgh and taught for a short time in secondary schools before taking up a lectureship in the University of Khartoum, Republic of the Sudan. He is now lecturer in English Studies at the University of Stirling. He is at present engaged in work on the modern poet Edwin Muir and the poetry of Shelley. He is the author of the York Notes on *Macbeth* and *The Waste Land*.

York Notes: list of titles

CHINUA ACHEBE
  Things Fall Apart
EDWARD ALBEE
  Who's Afraid of Virginia Woolf?
ANONYMOUS
  Beowulf
  Everyman
W. H. AUDEN
  Selected Poems
JANE AUSTEN
  Emma
  Mansfield Park
  Northanger Abbey
  Persuasion
  Pride and Prejudice
  Sense and Sensibility
SAMUEL BECKETT
  Waiting for Godot
ARNOLD BENNETT
  The Card
JOHN BETJEMAN
  Selected Poems
WILLIAM BLAKE
  Songs of Innocence, Songs of Experience
ROBERT BOLT
  A Man For All Seasons
HAROLD BRIGHOUSE
  Hobson's Choice
ANNE BRONTË
  The Tenant of Wildfell Hall
CHARLOTTE BRONTË
  Jane Eyre
EMILY BRONTË
  Wuthering Heights
ROBERT BROWNING
  Men and Women
JOHN BUCHAN
  The Thirty-Nine Steps
JOHN BUNYAN
  The Pilgrim's Progress
BYRON
  Selected Poems
GEOFFREY CHAUCER
  Prologue to the Canterbury Tales
  The Clerk's Tale
  The Franklin's Tale
  The Knight's Tale
  The Merchant's Tale
  The Miller's Tale
  The Nun's Priest's Tale
  The Pardoner's Tale
  The Wife of Bath's Tale
  Troilus and Criseyde
SAMUEL TAYLOR COLERIDGE
  Selected Poems
SIR ARTHUR CONAN DOYLE
  The Hound of the Baskervilles
WILLIAM CONGREVE
  The Way of the World
JOSEPH CONRAD
  Heart of Darkness
STEPHEN CRANE
  The Red Badge of Courage
BRUCE DAWE
  Selected Poems
DANIEL DEFOE
  Moll Flanders
  Robinson Crusoe
WALTER DE LA MARE
  Selected Poems
SHELAGH DELANEY
  A Taste of Honey
CHARLES DICKENS
  A Tale of Two Cities
  Bleak House
  David Copperfield
  Great Expectations
  Hard Times
  Oliver Twist
  The Pickwick Papers
EMILY DICKINSON
  Selected Poems
JOHN DONNE
  Selected Poems
GERALD DURRELL
  My Family and Other Animals
GEORGE ELIOT
  Middlemarch
  Silas Marner
  The Mill on the Floss
T. S. ELIOT
  Four Quartets
  Murder in the Cathedral
  Selected Poems
  The Cocktail Party
  The Waste Land
J. G. FARRELL
  The Siege of Krishnapur
WILLIAM FAULKNER
  The Sound and the Fury

HENRY FIELDING
Joseph Andrews
Tom Jones

F. SCOTT FITZGERALD
Tender is the Night
The Great Gatsby

GUSTAVE FLAUBERT
Madame Bovary

E. M. FORSTER
A Passage to India
Howards End

JOHN FOWLES
The French Lieutenant's Woman

JOHN GALSWORTHY
Strife

MRS GASKELL
North and South

WILLIAM GOLDING
Lord of the Flies
The Spire

OLIVER GOLDSMITH
She Stoops to Conquer
The Vicar of Wakefield

ROBERT GRAVES
Goodbye to All That

GRAHAM GREENE
Brighton Rock
The Heart of the Matter
The Power and the Glory

WILLIS HALL
The Long and the Short and the Tall

THOMAS HARDY
Far from the Madding Crowd
Jude the Obscure
Selected Poems
Tess of the D'Urbervilles
The Mayor of Casterbridge
The Return of the Native
The Woodlanders

L. P. HARTLEY
The Go-Between

NATHANIEL HAWTHORNE
The Scarlet Letter

SEAMUS HEANEY
Selected Poems

ERNEST HEMINGWAY
A Farewell to Arms
The Old Man and the Sea

SUSAN HILL
I'm the King of the Castle

BARRY HINES
Kes

HOMER
The Iliad
The Odyssey

GERARD MANLEY HOPKINS
Selected Poems

TED HUGHES
Selected Poems

ALDOUS HUXLEY
Brave New World

HENRIK IBSEN
A Doll's House

HENRY JAMES
The Portrait of a Lady
Washington Square

BEN JONSON
The Alchemist
Volpone

JAMES JOYCE
A Portrait of the Artist as a Young Man
Dubliners

JOHN KEATS
Selected Poems

PHILIP LARKIN
Selected Poems

D. H. LAWRENCE
Selected Short Stories
Sons and Lovers
The Rainbow
Women in Love

HARPER LEE
To Kill a Mocking-Bird

LAURIE LEE
Cider with Rosie

CHRISTOPHER MARLOWE
Doctor Faustus

HERMAN MELVILLE
Moby Dick

THOMAS MIDDLETON *and*
    WILLIAM ROWLEY
The Changeling

ARTHUR MILLER
A View from the Bridge
Death of a Salesman
The Crucible

JOHN MILTON
Paradise Lost I & II
Paradise Lost IV & IX
Selected Poems

V. S. NAIPAUL
A House for Mr Biswas

ROBERT O'BRIEN
Z for Zachariah

SEAN O'CASEY
Juno and the Paycock

GEORGE ORWELL
Animal Farm
Nineteen Eighty-four

JOHN OSBORNE
Look Back in Anger
WILFRED OWEN
Selected Poems
ALAN PATON
Cry, The Beloved Country
THOMAS LOVE PEACOCK
Nightmare Abbey and *Crotchet Castle*
HAROLD PINTER
The Caretaker
SYLVIA PLATH
Selected Works
PLATO
The Republic
ALEXANDER POPE
Selected Poems
J. B. PRIESTLEY
An Inspector Calls
WILLIAM SHAKESPEARE
A Midsummer Night's Dream
Antony and Cleopatra
As You Like It
Coriolanus
Hamlet
Henry IV Part I
Henry IV Part II
Henry V
Julius Caesar
King Lear
Macbeth
Measure for Measure
Much Ado About Nothing
Othello
Richard II
Richard III
Romeo and Juliet
Sonnets
The Merchant of Venice
The Taming of the Shrew
The Tempest
The Winter's Tale
Troilus and Cressida
Twelfth Night
GEORGE BERNARD SHAW
Arms and the Man
Candida
Pygmalion
Saint Joan
The Devil's Disciple
MARY SHELLEY
Frankenstein
PERCY BYSSHE SHELLEY
Selected Poems
RICHARD BRINSLEY SHERIDAN
The Rivals

R. C. SHERRIFF
Journey's End
JOHN STEINBECK
Of Mice and Men
The Grapes of Wrath
The Pearl
LAURENCE STERNE
A Sentimental Journey
Tristram Shandy
TOM STOPPARD
Professional Foul
Rosencrantz and Guildenstern are Dead
JONATHAN SWIFT
Gulliver's Travels
JOHN MILLINGTON SYNGE
The Playboy of the Western World
TENNYSON
Selected Poems
W. M. THACKERAY
Vanity Fair
J. R. R. TOLKIEN
The Hobbit
MARK TWAIN
Huckleberry Finn
Tom Sawyer
VIRGIL
The Aeneid
ALICE WALKER
The Color Purple
KEITH WATERHOUSE
Billy Liar
EVELYN WAUGH
Decline and Fall
JOHN WEBSTER
The Duchess of Malfi
OSCAR WILDE
The Importance of Being Earnest
THORNTON WILDER
Our Town
TENNESSEE WILLIAMS
The Glass Menagerie
VIRGINIA WOOLF
Mrs Dalloway
To the Lighthouse
WILLIAM WORDSWORTH
Selected Poems
WILLIAM WYCHERLEY
The Country Wife
W. B. YEATS
Selected Poems

York Handbooks: list of titles

YORK HANDBOOKS form a companion series to York Notes and are designed to meet the wider needs of students of English and related fields. Each volume is a compact study of a given subject area, written by an authority with experience in communicating the essential ideas to students at all levels.